JOHN DONNE:
A STUDY OF HIS
DRAMATIC IMAGINATION

V.N. Sinha, M.A., Ph.D.
Department of English,
Sana'a University
Yemen Arab Republic

Price 3.00

Printed in India by K.K. Bhargawa at The Caxton Press (P) Ltd.,
New Delhi.

CONTENTS

CONTENTS

PREFACE

The present work, originally submitted to the Banaras Hindu University as my doctoral dissertation, is a study of Donne's poetry from a special perspective, namely, of his dramatic imagination, This is, I wish to assert, an essential of his poetry and explains his creative mode. Without it his poetry loses much of its significance. Donne was a prolific writer. He wrote poems of a wide variety, such as *Songs and Sonnets, Elegies, Satires*, verse letters, philosophical poems like the *Anniversaries, Epicedes* and *Obsequies*, and *Divine Poems*. The study illustrates the dramatic mode of Donne's imagination through a sizeable and effective data, namely, the *Satires, Elegies,* and *Songs and Sonnets*. This involves some eighty poems, in the exegesis of which the fundamental point reveals itself.

It is hoped that my setting up of a schematic framework of dramatic imagination in poetry in general and in Donne's poems in particular, and detailed analyses of his poems, will provide students of Donne a much needed wider perspective and enable them to respond to his poems—their themes and techniques—with greater pleasure as well as benefit. The success of the work will, of course, depend upon the extent to which it satisfies the singularly marked enthusiasm of scholars of Donne even now.

I am indebted to the wide Donne scholarship which helped me in the formulation of my own perspective. I wish to thank Dr. A.P. O'Brien (formerly Professor of English and Head of the Department of English Studies, Banaras Hindu University), supervisor of my doctoral work, for his valuable suggestions on a number of points. I must olso acknowledge the valuable assistance I got from Dr. K.S. Misra (Head of the Deparment of English, Sana'a University) in the preparation of the final manuscript.

Sana'a, Y.A.R.   V.N. Sinha
1977

CHAPTER I

Critical Trends and Perspective

I

John Donne (1572-1631) has been studied widely as well as intensively in the twentieth century. A good deal of scholarship has been devoted to him and his poetry has been examined and re-examined to get the interrelations of poem and poem or a group of poems; and attempts have been made to define and assess Donne's sensibility and his poetic process. The differences and distinctions of the findings of critics have led to various theories, several of which are even in antithesis or in contradiction to each other. In this chapter a critical evaluation of some of the major trends in Donne criticism has been made in order to find what is tenable and what is not, or what is valid and what is not, in their view points. Inevitably, one is led, as this work will demonstrate, to the discovery of a major perspective or a compositional centre in each poem or sets of poems around which the poet's genius and poetry grew.

Broadly we have two distinct trends in the twentieth-century criticism of Donne, one which appeared early in the century during inter-war years with T.S. Eliot as the representative, and the other in the forties and after of which Rosemond Tuve was one of the chief early exponents. Their pioneering explorations and findings have been subject to revision and modification by other inquiring and perceptive scholars. The following paragraphs contain a critical survey of all these critics in quest of principles and correlations beyond them.

II

T.S. Eliot, representing the first trend, gave a new alignment to the study of Donne and Jacobean poets in his essays on "The Metaphysical Poets" (1921) and "Andrew Marvell" (1921). He did so by stating in the first that Donne was a modern poet in the way of modern French poets, for his poetry was a 'difficult poetry such as our complex civilisation demands.'[1] In his essay on "Donne in Our Time" (1931), Eliot experienced a change even as he did in his views of Milton and Shelley, and asserted that Donne was not a 'modern' in the modern sense of the word.[2] But in the earlier essays on Donne and the metaphysical poets he interpreted Donne as a modern, through shades of argument, for his 'heterogeneity of material compelled into unity by the operation of the poet's mind', 'fidelity to thought and feeling', and 'direct sensuous apprehension of thought, or recreation of thought into feeling.'[3] In his 1923 essay on "John Donne", Eliot again dwelt upon the modernity of Donne and paid him high tribute for his faithful portrayal of 'complicated states of mind' and for the 'potential or actual wit' that his poetry had everywhere. Donne's psychological realism and wit were explained as the reasons for the modern enthusiasm for him.[4] Donne was thus made what an ideal modern poet should be: an explorer of his own direct experience in a complex creative process.

How completely Eliot believed the capacity for 'a direct sensuous apprehension of thought, or a recreation of thought into feeling' to be the only right state for the mature poet (which he believed Donne was) is emphasised by his extended comment that :

When a poet's mind is perfectly equipped for its work, it is constantly amalgamating disparate experience; the ordinary man's experience is chaotic, irregular, fragmentary. The latter falls in love, or reads Spinoza, and these two experiences have nothing to do with each other, or with the noise of the typewriter or the smell of cooking; in the mind of the poet these experiences are always forming new wholes.[5]

In his essay on Marvell, the wit of the metaphysical poets is described as involving 'probably, a recognition, implicit in the expression of every experience, of other kinds of experience which are possible.'[6] The absence of this wit, a perpetual awareness of other possible experiences besides the one actually being expressed, and consequent unwillingness to express what the author has more immediately in mind either too lightly or too seriously the absence of this wit, this balance, this comprehensiveness, is what Eliot most deplored in the work of Milton and later poets; and in order to account for its absence he invented what has turned out to be one of the most famous phrases of modern English criticism, namely, 'dissociation of sensibility.'[7]

It is significant that of all of T.S. Eliot's essays on Donne and the metaphysical poets, the first two, ''The Metaphysical poets'' and ''Andrew Marvell'', both published in 1921, exerted a decisive influence on the subsequent criticism of Donne.[8] These two essays, in an attempt to define metaphysical and Caroline poetry, put forward some seminal ideas which were taken up by other critics with warm acceptance. Besides perpetuating T.S. Eliot's theory of Donne as a 'modern', critics like William Empson and Cleanth Brooks applied the new critical technique of linguistic analysis to the poetry of Donne and accepted Eliot's theory of 'heterogeneity of material compelled into unity by the operation of the poet's mind.' This cogently fitted their definitions of poetry as a language of ambiguity, and 'language of paradox.'[9] Even so formidable a critic as F.R. Leavis whose differences with T.S. Eliot were sharp, as is evidenced by *The Common Pursuit*,[10] in 1933 and again in 1935, supported the earlier Eliot stand on the metaphysicals when Eliot himself had moved away from his position of the 1921 essays. In a number of *Scrutiny* in 1933 F.R. Leavis wrote how Eliot's creative achievement had given his critical utterances their conclusiveness:

> The irresistible argument was, of course, Mr. Eliot's creative achievements; it gave his few critical asides—potent, it is true, by context,—their finality and made it unnecessary to elaborate a case.[11]

In 1935, Leavis wrote again, this time specifically on Eliot's views in the two essays on the metaphysical poets and Andrew Marvell. He wrote of the legislative nature of Eliot's views on them:

> Mr. Eliot's achievement is matter for academic evaluation, his poetry is accepted, and his early observations on the Metaphysicals and Marvell porvide currency for university lectures and undergraduate exercises.[12]

F.O. Matthiessen's view of Donne is an example of how Eliot's statements were extended by other critics who followed him. Viewing Donne as a modern involved in complex creativeness, Matthiessen stated:

> The jagged brokenness of Donne's thought has struck a responsive note in our age, for we have seen a reflection of *our own problem* in the manner in which his passionate mind, unable to find any final truth in which it could rest, became fascinated with the process of thought itself....What he strove to devise was a medium of expression that would correspond to the *felt intricacy* of his existence, that would suggest by sudden contrast, by harsh dissonances as well as by harmonies, the actual sensation of life as he himself had experienced it....His great achievement lay in his ability to convey his genuine whole of tangled feelings....'[13]

III

The other trend in the twentieth-century criticism of Donne began as a reappraisal of his poetry by historically oriented critics. In *Elizabethan and Metaphysical Imagery* (1947), bearing the sub-title "Renaissance Poetic and Twentieth-Century Critics", Rosemond Tuve completely rejected the stand that Donne was a modern and objected to the perspective of the poet so pronounced in Eliot and others like him. She wrote with irony of the modern critical attempts to endow the metaphysicals with aims more congenial to modern thinking and thus to bring them 'into the fold of adult sensitive moderns', and put it down as 'a form of buttering their hay.'[14] Distinguishing Donne's *Interpretation* as controlling subject' from 'the modern author's portrayal of his own process of interpreting or feeling, of "the very movement of thought in a living mind," the "interplay of perception and reflection," ' she said:[15]

> The earlier author's subject was different, however similar his stuff; his subject was still 'his meaning,' not 'himself-seeing-it'....Eliot shows us a man having a thought. Donne arranges the thoughts a man had...[16]

She rejected outright Eliot's concept of 'direct sensuous apprehension of thought' which had come to be used by modern criticism 'almost as an explanation of the peculiar nature of Metaphysical poetry', because it would have been found by any Elizabethan or Jacobean 'obscure and psychologically untenable.' She suggested the kind of approach desired for a correct study of Donne:

> ...interpretation of Donne by earlier poetic would have the advantage of removing from that keen critical mind the stifling seriousness about the experiences of his own consciousness with which most modern comment has cloaked it.[18]

The perspective of Rosemond Tuve was historical. She argued that the metaphysical poets must be evaluated in terms of their own times or according to Renaissance poetics and standards. The Renaissance critical theory, she claimed, provided a much more useful basis, not only for a study of the poetry of Donne, but for all poetry down to the Restoration. It explained the nature of his imagery and its relation to concepts and knowledge beyond and outside the personal experience of the poet and integrated that to his poems. Poetry to the Renaissance was an act of will and judgement, or as Rosemond Tuve has written: a 'willingness to include overt statement of meanings, and to supply clear directive phrases articulating the images with the rest of the structure.'[19]

Another feature cf the Renaissance poetics indicated by Rosemond Tuve was its quest in poetry for formal beauty. This meant a well-wrought poem, the form and the parts of which depended on rhetoric. Though rhetoric was not the sole instrument for achieving pure formal beauty, it had 'the most immediately distinguishable effect.' Tuve explained this when she wrote:

> ...design given to the natural (otherwise inadequately expressive), through the admirable craftmanship of the maker; and men of the Renaissance, like their predecessors, thought of the discipline of rhetoric as affording the poet necessary training in this respect.[20]

The enhancement of eloquence through rhetorical skill made poetry 'artificial' and carefully patterned.

Rosemond Tuve went on to observe that the Renaissance poetics regarded the function of poetry as didactic. This interconnected all the three learnings of rhetoric, poetry, and logic. 'The laws of logic were the laws of thought and the poet must know and use them; he will not otherwise be able to approach truth or direct the mind of man toward it.'[21] The second of the two parts of *Elizabethan and Metaphysical Imagery* related Renaissance poetry to the Renaissance logical method, suggesting in particular the link between metaphysical poetry and the rise of the new Ramist logic with its emphasis on dialectic, not merely for disputing or proving, but as a means of investigating the nature of things—of intellectual probing. This accounted for the emphasis on certain kinds of poetic methods that we are accustomed to call metaphysical; and Donne was 'the strictest poet-logician of his times.'[22]

Likewise, many other critics have, in reaction against the great enthusiasm for Donne's modernism which culminated in the years between the two world wars, sought to place him against the background of his own age and its habits of thought in order to qualify the importance and range of his poetry. A.J. Smith recommended a study of the Renaissance poetics and its great tradition of 'wit' (as it was developed in conventional rhetoric) for a true understanding of the qualities and techniques of Donne's poetry.[23] In absence of this, he said, Donne's poems and his technique alike would remain enigmatic, however sensitively handled, to our time which had sought their explanation in obscure states of mental tensions or lost conditions of sensibility; whose most cherished critical canons, indeed, had expressly repudiated any resort to extraneous circumstances.[24] The very title of J.B. Leishman's book on Donne, *The Monarch of Wit*, suggested a rejection of the idea of 'Donne the modern.' In the first chapter of the book Donne was set in the context of his English background. J.B. Leishman's point was that it was 'worthwhile to try to consider Donne more as a typical seventeenth-century or "strong-lined" poet...'[25] F.M. Kuna, in his essay on "T.S. Eliot's Dissociation of Sensibility and the Critics of Metaphysical Poetry", indicated the essential differences between the metaphysical and the modern styles and disapproved of the critical device suggested by G. Williamson of reading Baudelaire before studying Donne as extremely misleading. He related the style of Donne to the habit of thought prevailing in his age, which was one of analogy; of discovering and expressing the analogies binding the universe together.[27]

IV

The basic assumption of the earlier twentieth-century criticism of Donne is the present significance of literary works written in the past. It treats Donne as significant to the needs of the interests and concerns of its own time. The conditions prevailing in the twenties, which experienced a sharp and tremendous increase in the general interest in Donne, are important to note. The similarities between T.S. Eliot on Donne and the other critics of the inter-war years writing on the same subject are reflections of the common interests and the general consciousness of the period. Almost all Donne critics of the twenties and the thirties have one thing in common, a frank and direct interest in human experience. To them Donne appeared fresh and authoritative because his poems achieve that precious artistic illusion of a sense of real life, 'a sense of *the immediate present*.'[28] To their generation, discarding old forms and looking at all forms with suspicion, Donne appeared as a rebel, one who could be their model for expressing experience apparently freed from the methods and formulations for controlling and understanding experience, although these methods and formulations are, of course, a part of the standard equipment of any age, past or present. The critics reacting against T.S. Eliot were partly right in considering his criticism of Donne and the metaphysical poets as 'workshop criticism': that is, when he wrote his essays on the metaphysical poets, he was thinking rather of his own poetry and of the re-evaluation of the past by a modern mind than of an objective appraisal of a poetry of the past.[29] As such his criticism of Donne, as well as that by other critics who have like him approached Donne in order to seek in his poetry significance for the needs of their own immediate concerns, may be regarded as having motives which are quite often personal, self-justifying, expedient, or obsessive. Such a criticism is frequently vitiated by personal distortions and so is open to the charge of subjectivism.

This is not to deny the validity of a criticism which attempts to find in a literature of the past significance for the present. Yet, clearly, asserting that one may find in a work of the past anything one wishes and considers oneself free, in fact, to remake it entirely, is a mistake. The actual achievements of a poet may, it is true, exceed his conscious intentions.[30] But this implies that a proper understanding of the actual achievement of the poet we are studying requires a knowledge of his conscious intentions. It is not much use discussing values, most of all unconscious ones, until it is known what the poet was trying to do consciously; and with this the critics belonging to the earlier trend seem to have never been much concerned. Briefly, their approach was unhistorical.

T.S. Eliot and others who regard Donne as a modern have fallen into the initial mistake of Dr. Johnson's illustrious description of the metaphysical process which speaks of the yoking of heterogeneous things by violence together.[31] Dr. Johnson committed the prime critical error of treating the poetry of an age quite different from his own as though it belonged to his own time. The idea of metaphysical poetry thus begotten has found a fertile growth in our own century. Confusion of periods, then, is at the root of the familiar notions of undissociated or unified sensibility, 'heterogeneity of material compelled into unity by the operation of the poet's mind', and 'direct sensuous apprehension of thought, or recreation of thought into feeling.' The simplest objection to these is that they do not wholly apply to a large part of

Donne's poetry. J.B. Leishman found these phrases on Eliot 'out of place' for the unserious poems of Donne.[32]

The idea of unified sensibility which is implicit in Eliot's essay on "The Metaphysical Poets" the capacity of the poet's mind to 'devour any kind of experience', however disparate, and to form a new whole—[33] alone seems adequate to the modern mind. The 'new whole' is the form, the pattern, the amalgamating of fragments by the magic of language. The new whole resulting from the concentration of a large number of experiences is reached by certain stylistic devices, such as symbolist techniques, obscurity as a structural element, and fragments whose connection is not obvious but merely suggested. This is best seen in the words of Matthiessen. Drawing a parallel between the Symbolists and the Metaphysicals, he says:

> In both schools there is the demand for compression of statement, for centring on the revealing detail and eliminating all inessentials, and thus for an effect of comprehensiveness to be gained by the bringing to bear of a great deal of packed experience onto a single moment of expression.[34]

But such a parallelism ignores some essential differences between the metaphysical and the modern styles. The problem of unification of sensibility, F.M. Kuna says, did not exist for Donne. T.S. Eliot's theory appears to him 'a classical example of unhistorical thinking.'[35] The problem for Donne was one of correspondence which is achieved by logic and argumentation.

It seems from the frequent recurrence of the word 'sensibility' in "The Metaphysical Poets" that Eliot's regard for feeling overshadows that for thought. Bateson feels it is so.[36] But Donne's poetry is too intellectual to be described by the word 'sensibility' alone. Clay Hunt has many reservations about the unification of sensibility ascribed by Eliot to Donne. He finds Donne incapable of assimilating every kind of experience.[37] In Donne, he says, we do not have in any real sense (other than the literary device of analogy) a unity of the two words of thought and sense, abstract and concrete, intellectual and physical. The medieval conception of the social order, which regarded the universe as a highly articulated organism of members contributing in their different degrees to a spiritual purpose, was shattered, and differences which had been distinctions within a larger unity were now set in irreconcilable antagonism to each other. T.S. Eliot himself, in his 1931 essay on "Donne in Our Time", distinguishing Donne's sensibility from that of the Schoolmen who always aimed at 'unification: a *summa*', discovers in the former 'a manifest fissure between thought and sensibility.'[38] Donne's *Anatomy of the World* (*First Anniversary*) articulates the schism of the psyche (the 'dissociation of sensibility') between the two realms of the abstract and the sensible. The bringing together of two disparate realms is supposed to represent a unification of sensibility. It could more accurately be regarded as an artifice (in the course of its history running eventually to completely irresponsible extravagance) which attempts to make some unification between two divided realms; and the very act testifies, not to the 'unified' condition, but to the need for it and lack of it.[39]

The 'direct sensuous apprehension of thought' alone, though prominent in Donne, is insufficient to describe his poetry. This quality of Donne's apprehension is emphasized by Eliot elsewhere too. In his Clark Lectures he says:

I take as metaphysical poetry that in which what is ordinarily apprehensible only by thought is brought within the grasp of feeling, or that in which what is ordinarily only felt is transformed into thought without ceasing to be feeling.[40]

Mario Praz has indicated the singular likeness between this definition and the one given by Professor Martino of Baudelaire's inspirations in *Parnasse et Symbolism* (Paris, 1925).[41]

On the other hand, the critics reacting against the earlier trend in Donne criticism in the twentieth century based themselves on historical scholarship in order to keep aloof from the distractions of their own time and think themselves back to the historical sources of Donne's poetry. They approach the problems raised by his poetry from the perspectives offered by the sixteenth - and seventeenth-century literary critics themselves or by the actual literary practices of their centuries. There can be no basic objection to such an approach, and a critic as balanced and undogmatic as Helen Gardner has approved this development and its rejection of 'Donne the modern'.[42]

The main point raised by Rosemond Tuve and the critics with historical bent is that Donne's poetry should be read in the context of the later Renaissance. But, clearly, the problem cannot be solved by just trying to turn ourselves into seventeenth-century readers. This kind of transference or closing of distance cannot be fully done by a modern reader. 'I am convinced,' D.C. Allen says,

> that it is impossible to read a poem as a contemporary of the poet might have read it. One can explain lost references, one can annotate the poem from the historical remnants of its generation, but this is not giving it a contemporary reading. If we are told, 'Let us read this poem as a contemporary', we might ask which contemporary the reader has in mind. Since I cannot come close to reading an Elizabethan as an Elizabethan could, I can hardly have the bad taste to argue that I know how Spenser, Shakespeare, or Marvell wrote a poem.[43]

Further, the ultimate effect of a poem is above all a matter of the reader's response. He starts from where he is and what experience and information he possesses; he should correct continually by the acquisition of any knowledge that seems relevant, including that of the first reader's mental habits and the author's probable intention.[44] But along with these, he has also to open himself as best as he can to the impact of the total sum of all the parts of the poem. In absence of the last, a mere dependence on the habits of thought of the first readers and the author's probable intention will succeed at most in producing just an endorsement of the same habits and intentions. When a critic reads a work of the past against the background of the thoughts of that time and claims that he has found the truth about his subject because he knows the mental habits and intentions behind it, he is producing just such an endorsement, what A. Stein calls 'approaching idolatory.'[45]

The main question raised by the critics whose perspective is historical is how far the meaning of words in such poetry as Donne's is meant to be narrowed. It is impossible to make any simple generalisation about the extent to which we may extend the meaning of Donne's poems, for the situation varies from one poem to another. Clearly, a ground for the widening suggested above is provided by the Renaissance critics themselves, in their emphasis on dissimulating figures which work by doubleness. Puttenham defines the ways of figurative conveyance as 'a duplicity of meaning or dissimulation,' because 'they pass the ordinary limits of common utterance, and be occupied of purpose to deceive the ear and also the mind, drawing it from plainness and simplicity to a certain doubleness...' and are 'ways seeking to inveigle and apassionate the mind.'[46] If we remember this, Rosemond Tuve's contention that owing to Donne's complete command of the rhetorical instrument it is particularly 'illegitimate' in his case 'to fit out his poems with overtones which divulge ambiguously from his apparent meaning and which are only to be traced in the connotations of his image-terms'[47] must not but appear as a case of 'approaching idolatory.' And so also would it be if we accepted the probable effects of the Renaissance rhetoric on the poetry of the time[48] as the whole achievement of Donne. If it were accepted that Donne was only making a particularly stringent use of rhetoric devices for 'the elaboration, the enlivening, of some stock theme by means of a virtuoso play of dialectical fireworks',[49] which implies total unseriousness, even though the contrary may be professed, our discussion of the poet would better close with the remark of A. Quiller-Couch's American friend that Donne suffered 'from a rush of brains to the head.'[50]

Indeed there is much in Donne's poetry to support the view that 'imitation' by his time was 'reduced . to the witty rehandling of stock properties':[51] his ingenious comparisons, analogies and arguments, his power—as it were—to keep going for so long on subjects one might have supposed very rapidly exhaustible, that we find in many of his *Elegies* and *Songs and Sonnets*. Even at the turn of the sixteenth century the native word 'wit' had been acquiring the meaning of 'ingenuity.'[52] When Sidney, in his *Apology for Poetry*, which he wrote about 1583, remarked that 'we know a playing wit can praise the discretion of an Ass, the comfortableness of being in debt, and the jolly commodity of being sick of the plague,'[53] he was certainly referring to wit as mere ingenuity—wit in the sense of the Italian *ingengo* and the Spanish *ingenio*. Various paradoxes and encomia, many of them translations, in which we find such wit, were published in England during the later sixteenth and seventeenth centuries. Their popularity is, as J.B. Leishman has remarked, an interesting and important commentary on one of the interpretations given to 'wit' by that age and on how seriously that age could devote itself to a kind of learned and ingenious game.[54]

But is Donne's poetry characterised by only this kind of wit? Did Thomas Carew have only intellectual jugglery in view when he acclaimed Donne as 'a King, that rul'd as he thought fit/The universal Monarchy of wit?'[55] It could hardly have been so, for to Abraham Cowley wit was a thing of 'a thousand different shades,' the very essence of poetic genius, an intangible mystery of which we can only ask:

> What is it then, which like the Power Divine,
> We only can by Negatives define?[56]

The relation between wit and ingenuity is evident in the *Elegies upon the Author* included in Grierson's *Donne's Poetical Works*. But poetic wit, although the faculty involved in it is the same as that in facetious wit, is not quite the same as mere ingenuity. Ingenuity of wit is an ingredient of Donne's poetry, sometimes indulged for its own sake, but usually it is an instrument of his poetic wit.

There was no break between wit and imagination in the sixteenth and seventeenth centuries. Wit was not merely quickness of mind or fancy in Hobbes's sense, but also phantasy or imagination which Puttenham made basic to 'the invented part of the mind.'[57] This identification of wit and imagination by the time of Donne has to be emphasised in order to press the need of a fresh orientation in Donne's criticism, which could go beyond stressing merely the facetiousness of his wit and his use of rhetorical and logical devices to a just recognition of his actual poetic achievement in a sense acceptable to both the Renaissance and our own time.

The Renaissance poetics realised the importance of the rhetorical devices of wit. The common Elizabethan approach to poetry was rhetorical, for as Bacon observed, there was no art of the imagination, but there was an art of language.[58] The rhetorical forms as distinct from the grammatical forms of language were elaborately analysed and applied in the Renaissance. In poetry they often attained the status of a formal device. They were commonly taken as evidence of the poet's wit; they were at least a means of analysing its form. Though we still await a full-scale analysis of the part played by the Renaissance art of rhetoric in forming the six-teenth- and seventeenth-century styles, its importance may be seen from the most well known art of poetry of the time Puttenham's *The Art of English Poesy* (1589). For him poetry was both 'musical speech' and 'set out with all manner of fresh colours and figures.'[59] Of the importance of Putten-ham's essay Sir John Harrington wrote:

> ...where, as it were, a whole recipe of poetry is prescribed, with so many new named figures as would put me in great hope in this age to come would breed many excellent poets.[60]

When Puttenham spoke of phantasy or imagination, he defined its figurative function in the poet. Hence its product was commonly analysed by means of rhetoric into various kinds of rhetorical wit. It is this point of view that turns our atten-tion to the importance of rhetorical devices in Renaissance poetry.

However, if the Renaissance poetics had an awareness of the importance of the rhetorical devices of wit, it attached even greater value to 'invention' and advocated a just coordination of the two. So we find George Gascoigne saying in *Certain Notes of Instruction* (1975) that the first rule for making a poem is 'to ground it upon some fine invention.' He further adds, 'It is not enough to roll in pleasant words, ...unless the Invention have in it also *aliquid salis*.'[61] Putten-ham was alert to the ways in which figures contribute to the excellence of invention.[62] For Puttenham, again, though he observed that poetry was not only a kind of expression but also a mode of persuasion, the smaller kind of poems were related to emotional causes and occasions.[63]

Poetry, as the Renaissance understood it, was an art of imitation, and not a mere empiric of sound and form or the refashioning of traditional material. According to Puttenham, 'A Poet is as much to say as a maker', and like God who creates without 'any pattern or mould', 'makes and contrives out of his own brain both the verse and matter of his poem, and not by any foreign copy or example, as doth the translator, who therefore may well be said a versifier, but not a poet.'[64] We may also refer to Sir Philip Sidney's distinction between the 'Rhetorician' or 'Logician' and the poet. All arts take the works of nature for their principal object, but whereas 'the Rhetorician and Logician, considering which in Nature will soonest prove and persuade, thereon give artificial rules, which still are compassed within the circle of a question, according to the proposed matter,' 'the Poet, disdaining to be tied to any such subjection, lifted up with the vigour of his own invention, doth grow in effect another nature...'[65]

The corrective value of the criticism which has set Donne's poetry against the background of his age's habits of thought cannot be denied. A great service rendered by such criticism is to offer a definite point of difference between seventeenth-century poets and romantic or modern poets: the latter believe in expressing their personality and therefore explore the unconscious, and we misread the earlier ones if we suppose these ideas present in them. In a broad way this is right. Whatever effect of simplicity, sensuousness, and passion may be found in their best works, the primary aim of Elizabethan poets was not spontaneous outpouring of emotion. Theirs was a conscious art, rhetorical in method, concerned above all to impose form and order upon experience, working equally through the sense, the emotions, and the reason, and directed (at least in theory) at the will. Wit and the play of mind, argumentation, and logical development were therefore not foreign to it; artifice and convention were accepted as natural and desirable. Another service rendered by the historical critics lies in their provoking more careful thought about the relation between metaphysical and Elizabethan poetry. Most of the earlier critical rehabilitation of the metaphysicals had been accomplished against a background of conventional taste inherited from the nineteenth century: the main task was to break down romantic prejudices against wit, conceits, and metrical irregularity. Therefore, less careful attention, perhaps, was paid to what differentiated the metaphysicals from their predecessors, and something of the older conception of the Elizabethan age as romantic in the nineteenth-century way, only more youthful and naive, survived in some early criticism of Donne.

But the final value of the findings made by critics such as Rosemond Tuve and A.J. Smith is doubtful. It is so on account of the too exclusive attachment of this criticism to conscious intentions, to what Donne thought he was doing and what the contemporary reader thought had been done— as deduced from the evidence of current theory. This exclusive focussing on intention and contemporary theory has the obvious danger of deflecting attention from the actual experience of and response to poetry, and gives the impression, even if the contrary may be professed, that Donne was, as his own age would say, a versifier, not a poet. His primary achievements, from the point of view adopted by the historically oriented criticism of Donne, are far-fetched analogy, thorough-going application of logic and argumentative techniques, and use of rhetorical devices. Objection to such criticism may be expressed very briefly. It tends, in the words of William Empson, to 'explain things away.'[66] It suggests, either explicitly or by implication, that as the Elizabethan art of poetry was highly conscious, Donne must be read only for his surface intentions; that he did not mean at all the kind of thing the earlier twentieth-century critics admired him for, because he thought he had only to be witty and apply the rules of rhetoric in a particularly rigorous and stringent manner. Preoccupied with only conscious intentions, it either ignores or minimises the possibility that behind the inadequate modern discovery of immediate experience in Donne's poetry there lay a genuine perception, so that there is often the suggestion, without direct statement, that the perception was false. This is hardly acceptable, for while some of the poems of Donne, his verse-letters for instance, may support such a conclusion, his lyrics, both secular and divine, and even his *Satires*, do frequently present an actual and immediate experience, not in the manner of modern poetry, but as Donne's contemporary drama presented actual and immediate experience.

The critical approach represented by Rosemond Tuve and other critics like her has in most cases ignored the changing attitude to literature at the turn of the sixteenth century, perhaps because it would support the perception of the earlier critics—of immediacy in Donne. The Renaissance poetic's emphasis on 'invention' or the importance of matter has already been alluded to. George Gascoigne, while echoing Horace, interpreted a true English attitude towards art by according 'pleasant words' and 'apt vocables' only derivative significance. Invention is what counts.[67] Sir Philip Sidney's conception was much the same: '...any understanding knoweth the skill of the Artificer standeth in that *Idea* of foreconceit of the work, and not in the work itself.'[68] His disregard for ornament is not disapproval, however. His intention is to emphasise the intrinsic difference between the true poet and the 'many versifiers that need never answer to the name of Poets.' Near the end of the century, the precedence of matter over manner became even more pronounced, and it is a demand of history that this phenomenon should be accepted as an influence, no less decisive than Renaissance poetics and other mental habits of the time, on Donne's artistic expression.

During the last quarter of the sixteenth century the new

style of Muretus, Lipsius, and Montaigne gained momentum against the established cult of Cicero.[69] The Ciceronian emphasis on form was challenged by the new emphasis on reality and individual experience. The Ciceronians, Bacon said, searched 'more after the choiceness of the phrase, and the round and clean composition of the sentence, and the sweet falling of the clauses... than after the weight of the matter.'[70] The new style, on the other hand, deliberately broke up the symmetry of Cicero, using, either separately or in combination, a 'curt, compressed, pointed manner, or a loose, intimate, pliable style meant to reveal the workings of the mind.[71]

This new style in prose, the forerunner of the later plain style, has been rightly seen as part of a movement which affected poetry, and, indeed, all the arts. The influences that formed a kind of prose adapted to the ear and mind of an age might also be expected to manifest themselves in the poetry of that time. We see this in Donne's poetry, and in the censure of external polish and internal emptiness by Jonson, Chapman, and Daniel.[72]

Here we have to take note of the impact of modernism upon madievalism as the peculiar character of Donne's time, for it not only accounts for the far-fetched nature of his analogies but also explains the new attitude to literature we have been discussing. 'The belief in correspondences,' says F.M. Kuna, 'had been lost but not the mode of thinking which had gone with it. It was only natural that this should have deteriorated to a mere hunting for analogies. And it was likely that the more scepticism and cynicism arose, the more extravagant the analogies would become.'[73] To the same source we may also trace the accumulating change in the intellectual attitude and the approach to experience at the time of Donne as also the general movement against the Ciceronian style. This is not to suggest anything so ridiculous as that there was a sudden and complete break between the Elizabethan and the Jacobean; but only that the gradual change in the intellectual atmosphere made easier the acceptance of a style better accommodated to the ear and mind of the time. Merely referring to Donne's learning to prove his medievalism is not enough. What is really important is his attitude towards this learning. He reflects the naturalism of the Renaissance in its appeal from reason to the critical perception of facts. He does not turn this into an argued philosophy, but there are clear indications that he stands for the freedom of the mind to seek in fact and experience the ultimate basis for the truth about the nature of things.[74] For the medieval mind, logic, based on *a priori* methods of thinking, opened the path to knowledge. But in the later Renaissance, when experiment and direct observation preparing the way for modern science, challenged the adequacy of these methods, the communication of immediate experience became more important than just beautiful or systematic expression of general ideas.

We cannot get a composite picture of Donne's poetry unless we combine, with the Renaissance poetics and the sixteenth-century tradition of wit, the change in literary attitude and style perceptible during the last years of the century. And we may be sure that the conscious artist that Donne was, he was aware of the principle behind his practice of conveying immediate experience which is his characteristic and most frequent style in his *Satires* and lyrics. Thus it is not surprising to find Croll writing of the Senecan prose style in terms that suggest a strong relationship with the style of Donne. The following passage could, for instance, very well be thought of as coming from an early twentieth-century critic of Donne like T.S. Eliot:

Their purpose was to portray, not a thought, but a mind thinking, or, in Pascal's words, *la peinture de la penses*. They knew that an idea separated from the act of experiencing is not the idea that was experienced.[75]

This may be to read Senecan prose with the same twentieth-century expectations as have been attributed to T.S. Eliot in his reading of the poetry of Donne. Nevertheless, even a critic like K.G. Hamilton, who believes that the changes of taste between the sixteenth and seventeenth centuries were relatively minor and superficial compared with the fundamental concepts of the nature and function of poetry that remained unchanged, accepts the merits of such a reading.[76] Even if it turns out to be in some ways a misreading, it may yet be significant. It is valuable because it focusses our attention on what is most important in Donne, his 'human and dramatic imagination' and his creation of the artistic illusion of immediacy in his poems.

Rosemond Tuve has argued to disprove the notion of the metaphysical revolt against Elizabethan conventions. Certainly many poets kept up something like the earlier style well into the reign of James I, and some even beyond it.[77] But it is idle to minimise the difference and even Rosemond Tuve is constrained to refer to the changed intentions attendant on the separation of some forms from music occurring around the time when Donne wrote his poems.[78] By pursuing the implications of her suggestions we may arrive at a complete picture of Donne's poetic achievement. But she has ignored it, because it does not support the point she intends to make: that the English poetic tradition is 'so much of a piece from Marlowe (or Wyatt) to Marvell';[79] and anything that disturbs the harmony of this pattern must be minimised and understated. The changed intentions attendant on the separation of some forms from music indicates a change in poetic climate; a changed attitude to experience and style to which reference has already been made. Briefly, this change was from the lyric in its 'etymological and particular' sense to the lyric in its 'associative and general' sense.[80] The two kinds have much in common, and quite naturally so, for in spite of all their evident contradictions the second grows out of the first. But a shift from the one to the other is a shift from the impersonal to the personal, from the simple and emotional to the complex and intellectual. Donne's poetry marks such a shift. It has many things in common with the poetry of his Elizabethan predecessors, but his tough intellectual quality, the vigorously personal and colloquial style of his poetry, his directness, economy, concentration, and realistic force, stand at a far remove from the Elizabethan lyric—from its directness of syntax and smooth development of word order which are the essentials of music poetry, its fluency and copiousness of language, and easy regularity of verse. To profess that Donne's and Elizabethan lyrics are all one piece would hardly be correct.

Some of Donne's poems were meant to be set to music,[81] but his poetry is mainly expressive of the new attitude that demanded separation of poetry from music. He voices the poet's mistrust of the musician. In *The triple Fool* he speaks of trying to control his emotion in verse:

> I thought, if I could draw my pains,
> Through Rime's vexation, I should then allay,
> Grief brought to numbers cannot be so fierce,
> For, he tames it, that fetters it in verse.

(11.8-11)

According to R.W. Ingram, the poem is 'an augury' to the nature of Donne's lyrics.[82] The musician enters as an artist of quite another sort from the poet: the latter is writing personally, attempting to fetter his meaning for himself, while the musician comes 'his art and voice to show' for the many. Donne is trying to bind his feelings within careful words; the singer seizes on the inherent emotion, imprisoned within poetry, and frees it. The poet may cynically call himself a third kind of fool, but the implication remains of there being two artists working for different ends, private and public.

Donne's poem is a commentary upon that 'whining verse' which is, by implication, the Elizabethan love lyric: it is such verse that the singer most eagerly appropriates. The newer verse of Donne is such an amalgam of emotion and meaning as to be beyond the power of the musician; the musician can only weaken it. Such changes cannot, by their nature, be neatly dated and demonstrated in single persons. But there are few poems before Donne's which are built on exactly his structure or interpretation.

V

But this is not enough. Donne turned from the older type of lyric that was popular with his Elizabethan predecessors and showed a predilection for a different kind of which the most distinguishing feature is the manifestation of the dramatic mode of the poet's imagination. Working within the Renaissance tradition he created a poetic structure suitable to this dramatic mode and this was his originality, which would be acceptable, not only to the poetic theory of his own day with its conviction of poetic freedom,[83] but also to our own varying norm in the twentieth century.

In her Introduction to *The Metaphysical Poets* (1961), Helen Gardner wrote of this with brevity:

But his [Donne's] strong dramatic imagination of particular situations transforms the lyric and makes a metaphysical poem more than an epigram expanded by conceits.[84]

She wrote of Donne's dramatic imagination in passing and gave it as a critical assumption or an axiom. Thirteen years earlier, Cleanth Brooks had written in *Modern Poetry and the Tradition* (1948) of the essential and apparent dramatic qualities of Donne's poetry: 'Donne's poems are dramatic—

not only fundamentally but on the most obvious level.'[85]
Before these two major critics there were others who had
also written of the dramatic nature of Donne's poems. Pierre
Legouis, for instance, in *Donne the Craftsman* (1928),
acknowledged the dramatic power of Donne's poetry,
because—

> ...it succeeds in creating a voluptuous atmosphere and cal-
> ling up in it two flesh-and-blood human beings who act in
> relation to each other. The impression of passionate reality
> made upon the reader results partly from the poet's artfully
> concealed art, an art that is nothing if not dramatic.[86]

This is, as is evident, but a cursory glance at the dramatic,
mingling the dramatic in a restricted manner with the reader's
response—all expressed in one breath. Though Legouis took
the epithet 'dramatic' eventually in more than one sense, he
studied only some of the *Songs and Sonnets* with a limited
criterion of the dramatic without any relation to Donne's
imagination which is essential to the being of many of his
poems. T.S. Eliot in his essay on "Donne in Our Time"
(1931), taking his cue from Legouis, went a step further in
pursuit of the dramatic in Donne and hinged his view on the
conversational nature of Donne's poetry. J.B. Leishman's
The Monarch of Wit (1954) explicated the dramatic quality
of Donne's poems, but the whole book has surprisingly only
one small paragraph on what constitutes drama. His main
contention is that whereas non-dramatic poetry is static,
dramatic poetry is dynamic.[88] In the book we find the term
'dramatic imagination',[89] but its constituent elements have
nowhere been described.

As we have seen, critics have touched the idea of the
dramatic or dramatic imagination in Donne without an exig-
esis of the fundamentals. This leaves scope for a new perspective and a fresh study of the dramatic imagination of

Donne. There is need of further exploration and entry into the ramifications of Donne's dramatic imagination, and what that complex constitutes, and how it is actually in operation in his poetry, obtaining for him a unique and major place in English poetry.

FOOTNOTES

1. *Selected Essays 1917-1932*, London, 1932, p. 275.
2. *A Garland for John Donne*, ed. T. Spencer, Cambridge, 1931, p. 9.
3. *Selected Essays*, pp. 269, 271, 272.
4. Published in *The Nation and the Athenaeum*, 1923. The relevant paragraph is quoted in A. Alvarez, *The School of Donne*, London, 1961, pp. 13-14.
5. ''The Metaphysical Poets'', p. 273. The modern predilection for the poet's awareness and reconciliation of contraries in order to make a new whole is also found in so many other critics. F.R. Leavis, in ''Imagery and Movement'', *Scrutiny*, vol. xiii, September 1945, p. 120, generalises that 'whenever in poetry we come on places of especially striking ''concreteness''... we may expect analysis to yield instances of the co-presence in complex effects of the disparate, the conflicting or the contrasting ; and of course he finds such concreteness in Donne. Also refer to I.A. Richards's theory of the poetry of 'inclusion' and 'synthesis' (*Principles of Literary Criticism*, London, 1955, second edition, pp. 249-252), and the approval of this theory by Cleanth Brooks in his examination of the use of metaphor by Donne and other metaphysical poets (*Modern Poetry and the Tradition*, London, 1948, pp. 49-50). According to J.B. Douds, in ''Donne's Technique of Dissonance'', *PMLA*, vol. lii, December 1937, p. 1061, 'dissonance' was 'a most serviceable instrument, in fact, a prime necessity—for expressing Donne's multiple sensibility, his complex moods, and the discords of his temperament.' Further, 'creation of a technique for rendering the complex moment of feeling was probably Donne's greatest contribution to English poetry.' See also H.W. Wells, chapter on ''Radical Image'' in *Poetic imagery Illustrated*

from Elizabethan Literature, 1924, especially p. 125 ; and Alice Brandenburg's "The Dynamic Image in Metaphysical Poetry", *PMLA*, vol. lvii, December 1942, pp. 1041-1043.

6. "Andrew Marvell", p. 289.
7. "The Metaphysical Poets", p. 274.
8. See J.B. Leishman, *The Monarch of Wit*, London, 1957, pp. 87-88.
9. W. Empson, *Seven Types of Ambiguity*, London, 1949 ; Cleanth Brooks, *The Well Wrought Urn: Studies in the Structure of Poetry*, London, 1948, chapter i, pp. 3-20.
10. F.R. Leavis, *The Common Pursuit*, London, 1962, pp. 9-32.
11. "Milton's Verse", *Scrutiny*, vol. ii, September 1933, p. 123.
12. "English Poetry in the Seventeenth Century", *Scrutiny*, vol. iv, December 1935, p. 236.
13. *The Achievement of T.S. Eliot*, London, 1937, p. 12. See also G. Williamson's *The Donne Tradition*, Masachusetts, 1930, pp. 48, 89 f. ; W.B. Smith's "What is Metaphysical Poetry?," *Sewanee Review*, vol. xlii, p. 263 ; Margaret Willy's "The Poetry of Donne : Its Interest and Influence Today", *Essays and Studies*, New Series, vol. vii, 1954, p. 91.
14. Rosemond Tuve, *Elizabethan and Metaphysical Imagery*, Chicago, 1961, pp. 382-383.
15. *Ibid.*, p. 44.
16. *Ibid.*, p. 96.
17. *Ibid.*, p. 95 n.
18. *Ibid.*, p. 175.
19. *Ibid.*, pp. 175-176.
20. *Ibid.*, p. 27.
21. *Ibid.*, pp. 283-284.
22. *Ibid.*, p. 354.
23. "An Examination of Some Claims for Ramism", *The Review of English Studies*, New Series, vol. vii, 1956, pp. 348-359 ; "New Bearings in Donne : *Air and Angels*", *English*, vol. xiii, 1960.
24. "New Bearings in Donne : *Air and Angels*", pp. 50-51.
25. *The Monarch of Wit*, p. 17.
26. *Essays in Criticism*, vol. xiii, 1963, pp. 243-249, 251.
27. *Ibid.*, pp. 246-249.
28. *The Achievement of T.S. Eliot*, p. 67.
29. In *The Revival of Metaphysical Poetry : The History of Style, 1800 to the Present*, Minneapolis, 1959, J.E. Duncan observes that in the 'Twenties T.S. Eliot did nothing except talking about his own poetry, or the poetry he wanted to write, in terms of metaphysical poetry.'

30. According to A.E. Rodway, in "The Truth of Fiction", *Essays in Criticism*, vol. viii, 1958, p. 414, merely intention, even if it is known, cannot be used as a 'touchstone of value' because 'what a writer achieves may be very different from what he intended.'

31. "Life of Cowley", *Lives of the English Poets*, ed. G.B. Hill, vol. i, Oxford, 1905, p. 20. See A.J. Smith, "New Bearings in Donne : Air and Angels", p. 49.

32. *The Monarch of Wit*, p. 87.

33. "The Metaphysical Poets", p. 273.

34. *The Achievement of T.S. Eliot*, pp. 16-18.

35. F.M. Kuna, p. 251.

36. "The Critical Forum", *Essays in Criticism*, vol. ii, April 1952, p. 214.

37. *Donne's Poetry*, New Haven, 1954.

38. "Donne in Our Time", pp. 7-9.

39. See H.W. Smith, "The Dissociation of Sensibility", *Scrutiny*, vol. xviii, 1951-52, pp. 175-188.

40. Quoted in Mario Praz's "Donne's Relation to the Poetry of his Time", *A Garland for John Donne*, p. 58. See also Margaret Willy's "The Poetry of Donne : Its Interest and Influence Today", p. 91.

41. "Donne's Relation to the Poetry of his Time", p. 59.

42. Introduction to *John Donne : A Collection of Critical Essays*, ed. Helen Gardner, New Jersey, 1962, p. 11.

43. Introduction to *Image and Meaning : Metaphoric Traditions in Renaissance Poetry*, Baltimore, 1960, p. vii.

44. R.G. Cox, "The New Scholarship?", *Scrutiny*, vol. xix, 1952-53, p. 83.

45. *John Donne's Lyrics : The Eloquence of Action*, London, 1962, p. 4.

46. "The Art of English Poesy", *Elizabethan Critical Essays*, ed. G. Smith, vol. ii, Oxford, 1904, pp. 160, 47-48, 169. See also Gascoigne in *Elizabethan Critical Essays*, vol. i, p. 47. A summary of John Hoskins's view of dissimulating figures can be found in G. Williamson's *The Proper Wit of Poetry*, London, 1951, pp. 14-25.

47. *Elizabethan and Metaphysical Imagery*, p. 213. An illuminating discussion of the problem is found in W. Empson's "Donne and the Rhetorical Tradition", *Kenyon Review*, vol. xii, 1949, p. 580.

48. "New Bearings in Donne : Air and Angels", pp. 49-51.

49. *Ibid.*, p. 50.

50. See also J. Smith's statement that if Donne 'merely plays ducks and drakes with ideas,' we may as well abandon our investigation: 'we shall find a perfectly satisfactory account of him in Johnson.' "On Metaphysical Poetry", *Scrutiny*, vol. ii, 1933, p. 224.

51. "New Bearings in Donne : *Air and Angels*", p. 50.

52. J.E. Spingarn, Introduction to *Critical Essays of the Seventeenth Century*, vol. i, Oxford, 1908, pp. xxix-xxx.

53. *Elizabethan Critical Essays*, vol. i, p. 181.

54. *The Monarch of Wit*, p. 77.

55. *An Elegy upon the Death of the Dean of Pauls. Dr. John Donne*, 11. 95-96.

56. *Ode; of Wit*, 1656, 11. 55-56.

57. *Elizabethan Critical Essays*, vol. ii, 19-20.

58. Bacon in *The Advancement of Learning* : 'in the first sense it is but a *Character* of style, and belongeth to Arts of speech...' *Critical Essays of the Seventeenth Century*, vol. i, p. 5.

59. *Elizabethan Critical Essays*, vol. ii, p. 8.

60. "A Brief Apology for Poetry", 1591. *Elizabethan Critical Essays*, vol. ii, p. 196.

61. *Elizabethan Critical Essays*, vol. i, pp. 47-48. According to Sir John Harrington, the two parts of poetry are 'invention of fiction and verse', and if the order in which he puts them is any indication, to him 'invention or fiction' was the more important. *Ibid*. vol. ii, p. 204.

62. *Ibid.*, vol. ii, p. 160.

63. *Ibid.*, p. 25.

64. *Ibid.*, p. 3.

65. *Ibid.*, vol. i, p. 156.

66. "Donne and the Rhetorical Tradition", p. 578.

67. *Elizabethan Critical Essays*, vol. ii, pp. 47-48.

68. *Ibid.*, p. 160.

69. See Croll's "Muret and the History of 'Attic' Prose", *PMLA*. vol. xxxix, p. 293 ; " 'Attic Prose' in the seventeenth century", *Studies in Philology*, vol. xviii, 1921, pp. 79-128 ; "The Baroque Style in Prose", *Studies in English Philology in Honour of Frederick Klaeber*, ed. Malone and Rudd, Minneapolis, 1929, pp. 427-56. See also George Williamson's "Senecan Style in the Seventeenth Century', *Philological Quarterly*, vol. xv, 1936, pp. 321-352 : "Strong Lines", *English Studies*, vol. xviii, 1936, pp. 152-159.

70. *Philosophical Works*, ed. Spedding, 1857, vol. iii, p. 283.

71. "The Baroque Style in Prose", pp. 452-453.

72. "From the *Conversation with Drummond*", *Critical Essays of the Seventeenth Century*, vol. i, p. 214; *Poems and Minor Translations*, 1875, p. 55; *Elizabethan Critical Essays*, vol. ii, pp. 364. 381.

73. F.M. Kuna, p. 246. See also W.J. Courthope's *A History of English Poetry*, London, 1911, vol. iii, pp. 147-148.

74. C.M. Coffin, *John Donne and the New Philosophy*, London, 1937, pp. 238-284,

75. "The Baroque Style in Prose", p. 430. See also F.P. Wilson's *Elizabethan and Jacobean*, Oxford, 1946, p. 26; Patrick Cruttwell's *The Shakespearean Moment*, London, 1954, pp. 89f; J.B. Leishman's, *The Monarch of Wit*, pp. 16-17, 157-158.

76. K.G. Hamilton, *The Two Harmonies : Poetry and Prose in the Seventeenth Century*, Oxford, 1963, p. 6.

77. R.G. Cox, "A Survey of Literature from Donne To Marvell", *From Donne To Marvell*, ed. Boris Ford, Harmonsworth, 1960, pp. 44-51. 84.

78. *Elizabethan and Metaphysical Imagery*, pp. 176, 198.

79. *Ibid.*, p. 351.

80. Catherine Ing, *Elizabethan Lyrics : A Study in the Development of English Metres and their Relation to Poetic Effect*, London, 1951, pp. 15-20.

81. *Ibid.*, p. 231.

82. R.W. Ingram, *Elizabethan Poetry*, London, 1960, pp. 145-147.

83. Gregory Smith, Introduction to *Elizabethan Critical Essays*, vol. i, p. xxv. According to David Klein, in *The Elizabethan Dramatists as Critics*, New York, 1963, p. 18, the Renaissance exemplified two trends in art criticism : 'the romantic, which gave precedence to imagination and freedom in art production, stemming from Plato, and the classic, which insisted on the dominance of reason and control, stemming from Aristotle.' The two were not disengaged from each other but usually went together.

84. Introduction to *The Metaphysical Poets*, London, 1959, pp. 22-23.

85. Page 208.

86. "The Dramatic Element in Donne's Poetry". *John Donne: A Collection of Critical Essays*, p. 41.

87. Page 16. Eliot has stated that the verse method of Donne is the same as of Browning, Lafourge, and Corbiere, 'either dramatic monologue or dialogue.'

88. Page 59. See also pp. 47-48 and 266 for the dramatic element in Donne's poetry.

89. *Ibid.*, p. 155.

CHAPTER II

The Dramatic Imagination

I

Any essay on the dramatic imagination, its nature and quality, has to start with a premise, namely, of the poetic imagination, and of other consequential factors as a second premise, vital to the act of creation and poetry. Imagination is the source of all poetry and by virtue of it whatever is given in perception can mingle with abstract concept and be submitted to conscious selection and criticism without losing its peculiar perceptual character—that is, without losing the charges of feeling it acquires in the act of perception.[1] This is the only satisfactory account of the commerce between percepts and concepts, and any adequate psychological theory of art must be based on this. In the imagination which creates poetry there is no chasm between perception and conceptual understanding. It is so in Coleridge's notion of imaginative synthesis, instantaneously interfused at the higher end with reason and at the lower end with the senses. Coleridge recognises the distinction and specifically draws attention to it within his own theory in the distinction between imagination and fancy in the thirteenth chapter of *Biographia Literaria*.[2] Fancy is 'the faculty of bringing together images dissimilar in the main by some one point or more of likeness'; the images of fancy are constructed by the exercise of will and logic, imagination, on the other hand, is 'the power by which one image or feeling is made to modify many others, and by a sort of fusion to force many into one; 'the images of imagination are constructed by an unwilled constellating process of memory, are richly toned with feeling, form and true syntheses by fusing themselves dynamically into each other and into their context. Finally, imagination, by 'combining many circumstances into one moment of consciousness, tends to produce that ultimate end of all human thought and human feeling, unity.'[3] The aesthetic sense may be defined, thus, in the most general meaning of the term, as the sense of order: the awareness of the culminating phase of an internal mental process tending one way, towards order and unity.

The associative link for fancy is always an idea, a *fixed* connection between counters, 'fixed and definite'; its images are static, toneless, decorative, stable, because they have been raised out of their experiential context and have lost the indeterminacy of outline and richness of meaning that intense feeling alone can give them. But the images of imagination are single, immediate, and singular; by sudden collision and fusions they bring out hitherto unrecognised relations. The feeling-tone or sensibility which typifies imagination is the sign, not only that the whole man is engaged, but also that here is an activity arising from an event of reality. *In The Poetic Pattern*, Robin Skelton stresses the 'subjective-objective quality of perceived unity' in poetry. In a rarely suggestive passage he has summed up the difference between fanciful and imaginative writings thus:

Fanciful writing is unified only by the existence of its separate elements in a three-dimensional world of actuality, while imaginative writing possesses the unity or a pattern of three-dimensional life seen clearly with the aid of a four-dimensional observer.[4]

D.G. James finds Kant's growing awareness of the imagination as the common root of both sensibility and understanding (see *Critique of Pure Reason*, tr. Norman Kemp Smith, 1929, p. 146. Also, *Commentary* on Kant's *Critique*, *Ibid.*, p. 225) more satisfactory than his earlier theory which gives, in many ways, a primary place to the understanding rather than to the imagination (the central passages on imagination, synthesis, and schemata are found in *Critique of Pure Reason*, pp. 112, 165, 182), because it indicates 'sensibility' as a form of activity without which we could not be aware of spatial and temporal order, and the understanding as conditioned upon the imagination for its operation. D.G. James favours 'the notion of a creative imagination operative in "sensibility".'

Even J.S. Mill, brought up in the eighteenth-century tradition and an associationist, not only recognised the value of Coleridge's theory as a necessary corrective, but wrote in "Thoughts on Poetry and its Varieties" (1859) that poets are those 'who are so constituted, that emotions are the links of association by which their ideas, both sensuous and spiritual, are connected together.'[6] He further added:

At the centre of each group of thoughts or images will be found a feeling; and the thoughts or images will be there only because the feeling was there. The combinations which the mind puts together, the pictures which it paints, the wholes which Imagination constructs out of the materials supplied by Fancy, will be indebted to some dominant *feeling*, not as in other natures to a dominant *thought*, for their unity and consistency of character, for what distinguishes them from incoherencies....the poetry of a poet is Feeling itself, employing Thought only as the medium of its expression.[7]

Understanding alone can only operate with elements that are already clear and constant, and all it can do is to arrange and reversibly rearrange these elements. It can give us an intellectually intelligible statement of a principle behind an experience, but it cannot provide us with a sense of the whole.[8] It can lead only to abstractions which are conceptual and devoid of feeling-tone—aptly described as 'the keystone to the aesthetic arch.'[9] The central term for tracing an unbroken creative process from the primal event of perception to the completed work of art is *feeling*, and in poetry feeling and memory combine in a process where analytical thinking plays only the marginal (though by no means insignificant) role of critic and casual stimulant.

What has been said so far is, however, not a negation of intellect in poetry. In our adult experience imaginative perception is seldom unaccompanied by intellectual processes. No normal man can reduce himself to a condition of thought-lessness. While discussing Kant's view of the relative importance of understanding and imagination, D.G. James remarks :

> The discursive operation of the intelligence effects its analysis of what is originally brought together by the imagination. But all our knowledge shows these two sides, the direct and the imaginative, prehending individual wholes; the reflective or discursive, analysing and classifying. They necessarily occur together in all adult experience; but they cannot be identified...[10]

It is the case, indeed, that these two elements are always present together in our knowledge of the world. But the distinction between the life of the imagination and the life of the intellect should be kept in mind. Whereas the life of the imagination consists in the perception of unity and individual wholes, the life of the intelligence consists in classification and abstraction.

Cleanth Brooks has criticised the romantics like Wordsworth and Coleridge for their suspicion of intellect in poetry.[11] and affirmed that 'the play of the intellect is not necessarily hostile to depth of emotion.'[12] Further, according to him, 'There are complex attitudes in which there is an interplay—even a swift interplay—of intellect and emotion; and these romantic critics neglect the possibility that levity itself may sometimes be used to intensify seriousness.'[13] Rightly so. The romantic suspicion of intellect in poetry is basically right, but it is to be observed that the romantics did not absolutely banish intellect from poetry. According to Wordsworth, of the several ingredients of poetry 'judgement' is one.[14] The term also finds a place in Coleridge's celebrated passage on the function of imagination in the fourteenth chapter of *Biographia Literaria*;[15]

[The poet] diffuses a tone and spirit of unity, that blends and (as it were) *fuses*, each into each, by that synthetic and magical power, to which I would exclusively appropriate the name of imagination. This power, first put into action by the will and understanding, and retained under their irremissive, though gentle and unnoticed control...reveals itself in the balance and reconcilement of opposite and discordant qualities: of sameness, with difference; of the general with the concrete; the idea with the image; the individual with the representative...a more than usual state of emotion with more than usual order; *judgement* [italics mine] ever awake and steady self-possession with enthusiasm and feeling profound or vehement...

This passage also clarifies Coleridge's phrase about the secondary imagination 'co-existing with the conscious will.'[16] He does not mean that the secondary imagination is 'co-extensive' with the conscious will, but rather that it cannot function without the infusion of will and understanding.

Coleridge has described the term imagination at two levels which he calls 'primary' and 'secondary'[17] (The one is a mode of image-making, a function of memory. The other is a transcendental activity which terminates in a poem whose constituent images are produced by a special mode of image making.) No matter how closely related the two processes may be—and indeed the second must flow seamlessly from the first—two distinct processes can and should be discerned. Imagination at the first level is the imagination operating at the most elementary level of the direct act of perception, organising whatever is perceived instantly into a meaningful pattern without the intrusion of analysis or thinking. At the second level, the imagination is engaged in a two-fold activity which resolves itself into a synthesis and integrated psychic unity. This activity is not a spontaneous mechanism, but 'co-exists with the conscious will.'

A poem springs from an event of knowing characterised by vivid perception, intense feeling, and a conviction of value. When such an event intrudes into consciousness, the associative function of memory which we call imagination is stimulated and orients itself in a particular manner. This kind of experience is a state of heightened feeling which is a state of disequilibrium. Equilibrium is established by channelising the energy of feeling into a corresponding rhythmic language. The poet achieves a sort of catharsis by imposing a form on his self-expression; a form which has grown out of the feeling and also encloses it. By transmuting the event of knowing into a poem, the poet passes from a state of tension to cathartic repose.[18] Thus the action of the poet is not an 'escape' but just the opposite—'inscape' or a particularisation,[19] for he resolves the heightened feeling by a closer identification with the event; by holding the event to himself he clarifies the feeling of that event as minutely and accurately as he can.[20]

II

The process we have been describing is, it may be assumed, largely unconscious. According to L. L. Whyte, the formative processes which involve the remoulding of pre-existing elements must take place outside the field of fully focussed attention. He observes:

A form in the brain-mind cannot be remoulded and clarified while it is the subject of concentrated attention; what is fully conscious must remain constant, as it were; the emergence of a new pattern, which depends on the modification of the old parts, must proceed unconsciously. True creation is always unconscious.[21]

Yet it is submitted that poetic creation is both unconscious and conscious. The secondary imagination is in fact, 'co-existing with the conscious will,' first brought into operation by the will and understanding. Indeed, it is from the balance of these opposites that poetry is born. The poetic process is not a purely mechanical and psychic process, for it always involves the person and not only an organism.[22] Accessible only to contemplation, value enters the process—if it is to enter at all—at the radical level of perception. And since this element of value must be sustained throughout the poetic process, the activity is inevitably centred upon the person. At no level is the process innocent of selection and direct judgement. Any particular cycle of the process, is what it is because it has occurred in this individual and unique person; not because he is an organism with certain peculiarities but because he is a person of unique nature, awareness, and concern.[23]

In the poetic activity, according to Robin Skelton, the unconscious and conscious minds appear to fuse together.[24] He has dwelt in some detail on the establishment of the poetic equilibrium in the tenth chapter of *The Poetic Pattern*. He refers to Louis Macniece's feeling that the poetic attitude is related to childhood, for the child operates as a unity and considers almost everything in terms of the personal. But the poet is more than the child. He achieves his equilibrium at a higher and more complex level. The conscious elements of his personality have developed through the process of individuation, and a longer experience of life has enlarged the amount of sense-data of which he can make use. Moreover, with the passage of years, more events have occurred in his psyche, and, though his instinct may be less clear and definite than that of the child, there has come to exist a greater degree of tension between his instinct and reason on account of the development of his personality. This results in the release of a greater amount of energy at moments of equilibrium. Of course, the degree of equilibrium varies from poet to poet. There can be either low or high tension poetry.

Two things seem certain about the composition of a poem:[25]

(i) There is the role of the unconscious (varying with poems), beyond the pale of literary criticism, in the making of every true poem. It is not only, as Robin Skelton remarks, that it is easy for a non-writer of poetry to appreciate the more conscious methods of writing.[26] The only sure grounds for criticism to tread upon are these, that is, the final stages of Whalley's 'symbolic extrication' in which the relevant images are evoked, selected, and articulated, under the government of two unifying principles: the single unifying passion which is the integrity of the event of reality, and a style which is the personal integrity of the poet.[27] What happens in the process before this belongs to the sphere of psychology. Criticism cannot look into the poet's mind; it can only attempt to infer activity from its physical manifestations in the poem. After admitting that much that goes to make a poem is unconscious, I.A. Richards warns that the mental processes of the poet are not a very profitable field for investigation.[28] The attempt to display the inner working of the poet's mind by the evidence of his work alone must be subject to the gravest dangers. The difficulty is that nearly all speculations as to what went on in the artist's mind are unverifiable.

(ii) At the same time, the resultant poem needs to be perfected by a more conscious use of the poet's critical faculty. We may cite the testimony of poets themselves. Robert Graves [29] admits that a poem worthy of the name is rhythmically formed in the poet's mind, during a 'trance-like suspension of his normal habits of thought,' by 'the supra-logical reconciliation of conflicting emotional ideas.' This is the preliminary process of composition. As soon as this is done, the secondary phase of composition begins; that of 'testing and correcting on commonsense principles, so as to satisfy public scrutiny, what began as a private message to himself from himself—yet taking care that nothing of poetic value is lost or impaired.' It appears that the final stages in the process of poetic creation are of groping towards the pattern perceived at the moment of inspiration. This aspect of the matter is further clarified by Stephen Spender in *The Making of a Poem*.[30] He describes how the first draft of a poem is 'like a face which one seems to be able to visualise clearly in the eye of memory, but when one examines it mentally or tries to think it out, feature by feature, it seems to fade.' Having given us the first draft of the poem, he proceeds to show the process of the secondary composition, what we have described as the *groping towards the pattern* perceived at the moment of inspiration: 'In the next twenty versions of the poem I felt my way towards the clarification of the seen picture, the music and inner feeling.' And this feeling his way by the poet towards the realisation of the original impulse is certainly conscious, though it is impossible even here to say how much. The art of some poets is more conscious, of others less. Ben Jonson, we might say, worked with greater self-consciousness and a higher sense of organisation than Shakespeare. There is more conscious cerebration in a poem by Eliot than in one by Coleridge, though both regard conscious volition as an essential of poetry. C. D. Lewis and George Whalley stress the will-lessness of the poet.[31] T.S. Eliot, Kenneth Burke, and Cleanth Brooks, on the other hand, though not denying the unconscious imaginative synthesis that occurs prior to its expression through proper symbols, words—in the case of poetry, emphasise the deliberateness of the poet's organisation.[32]

No rules can be prescribed, for the rules of imagination are, as Coleridge has remarked, themselves the laws of freedom and growth. We may only say, in the words of Robin Skelton:

> Over-addiction to the exploration and exploitation of the purely subjective aspects of experience, obsession with non-intellectual, non-logical processes of the subconscious, is as mistaken as over-intellectualisation or addiction to purely objective, mathematical, and definite ways of thought. The two must be combined, as in all good poems—certainly in the best of W.B. Yeats, Dylan Thomas, Wordsworth and Blake—they invariably are.[33]

Surely it was the same realisation that made Coleridge say: 'Imagination must have Fancy, in fact the higher intellectual powers can only act through a corresponding energy of the lower.'[34] I.A. Richards's interpretation is that under the checks of the senses and reason, of the activity of thought and the vivacity of the accumulative memory, the mind in its normal state uses *both* fancy and imagination.[35] Fancy and imagination are not exclusive of or inimical to each other. The making of a poem has a dynamic nature and reflects the dynamic nature of the poetic activity—the opposition of and the cooperation between opposites, the conscious and the supra-logical processes. It is thus that each poem dictates its own form.

III

The poetic process is one of dissipation of the feeling of unrest and inner disturbance arising from the obscurity of primary perceptions—by a more adequate self-consciousness. It is this objectification of the self which relates emotional and conative experiences and makes poetry possible. This being the case, there must go on a certain 'depersonalisation' in all poetry, whether lyrical or dramatic. In this sense, Shelley's *Lines Written in Dejection* is as objective as Shakespeare's *Othello*. Shelley's poem is subjective only in the sense that it happens to be concerned with an emotional state which actually occurred in the life of the poet. Aesthetically, however, this fact is irrelevant. Both lyrical and dramatic poetry express imaginative apprehension of some object, whether that object be the poet's own feelings, or some one else's, or a tree, or the moon. The poet apprehends his own self and feelings as he would an object external to him. There is at this level no essential difference of poetic process between lyrical and dramatic poetry.

The impersonality, which the poet must achieve in his work, should not be confused with a diminution of the life of feeling and action, 'a withdrawal, if such a thing were conceivable, from emotional experience and the strenuous practice of life.'[36] Edward Bullough is quite explicit on this point in his famous essay on " 'Psychical Distance' as a Factor in Art and an Aesthetic Principle."[37] After defining his concept of 'distance' as separation of the object and its appeal from one's own self, he says:

But it does not mean that the relation between the self and the object is broken to the extent of becoming 'impersonal'... On the contrary, it describes a *personal* relation, often highly emotionally coloured, but of a *peculiar character*. Its peculiarity lies in that the personal character of the relation has been, so to speak, filtered. It has been cleared of the practical, concrete nature of its appeal.

Impersonality, as enunciated above, is inevitably a feature of all poetry. As such the imagination behind dramatic poetry is no more detached or objective than the imagination in lyrical poetry. According to the foregoing argument, it follows that a distinction between dramatic and lyrical poetry on the ground that the one is more impersonal and objective than the other is fallacious.

In his celebrated essay on "Poetry",[38] W.T. Watts-Dunton distinguishes two types of poetic imagination, the '*absolute* dramatic vision' and the '*relative* dramatic vision.'[39] Later in the essay the two are described as the '*dramatic imagination*' and the '*egoistic imagination*' respectively.[40] The first is, in its highest exercise, 'unconditioned by the personal or lyrical impulse of the poet.' On the contrary, the second is 'more or less conditioned by the personal or lyrical impulse of the poet.' Elaborating the distinction further, Watts-Dunton adds that the former enables the poet to make 'special individual characters', other than his own, live in the imagined situation whereas the latter only enables the poet, even in its very highest exercise, to make his own individuality live in the imagined situation.[41]

The distinction, as made by Watts-Dunton and followed by Bliss Perry,[42] between lyrical and dramatic poetry, is unacceptable. It is doubtful whether the absolute vision or objectivity which they attribute to drama has ever been achieved by any dramatist, living or dead. In fact, such objectivity is hardly an ideal worth achieving in art. It belongs to the realm of abstract or pure science which alone is 'absolute' in the sense that it completely eschews the subjective. To say that drama possesses such objectivity is to distort the impersonality ascribed to drama and is a sort of over-simplification for the sake of theoretical distinction between dramatic and lyrical poetry. In both cases the poetic creation is a result of the poet's imaginative contemplation. It is not for the poet to represent things as they actually are but as his imagination perceives them. Egoism is a characteristic of all poets and not only of the lyric poet. But mere egoism cannot make poetry. The creation of poetry requires egoism to be imaginatively transformed. The 'I' of the lyric poet is filtered through imagination and hence in a degree is impersonalised as any character in drama.

C.S. Lewis has stated such a view in "The Personal Heresy in Criticism."[43] Although he has advanced the poetic impersonality to an extreme, he leaves us in no doubt about what we want to emphasise here. According to him, 'at best—we meet the poet, even in the most personal lyric poetry, only in a strained and ambiguous sense'; and it is, in fact, 'quite impossible that the character represented in the poem should be identically the same with that of the poet.'[44]

Stated in modest terms, the situation as described by C.S. Lewis comes to this. Self-expression as it happens in poetry is always, when successful, the expression of the creativeness of the imagination, and never merely of emotion. The poet writes about himself or any other object only to the extent that it is creative. Whether the subject of the poet is 'I', or a character other than his own, it is changed in and through the labour of self-expression. Imaginative contemplation of the self transforms the 'I', giving it the impersonality which belongs to characters avowedly different from the poet's. Thus, impersonality, as understood in the present discussion, is a necessary outcome of the poetic process.

Poetry, whether lyrical or dramatic, is both subjective and objective.[45] The poet proceeds to translate his perception into words partly by instinct, partly by following the tradition of his predecessors, but very largely by the method of trial and error; and the result, when it comes, is for him, no less than for us, an acquisition, a voyage beyond the limits of his personal point of view; an annihilation of the brute fact of his own particular psychology rather than its assertion. This applies to both the lyric poet and the dramatic poet. Conversely, the dramatic poet's mind is to him as much a 'kingdom' as the lyric poet's. Of both, and not only of the dramatic poet, the impulse is 'the simple yearning to create akin to that which made "the great Vishnu yearn to create a world." '[46] Both create imaginatively and it cannot be true that the characters of drama are absolutely independent of the poet who has created them. Coleridge has said of Shakespeare, who undoubtedly possessed 'dramatic imagination', that he 'becomes all things, yet for ever remaining himself.'[47] The poet's individuality, or 'personal or lyrical impulse', is present in dramatic poetry as well as lyrical poetry. In both cases, this individuality has to be transcended. T.S. Eliot's view of how a dramatist makes his characters 'vital' is relevant to our discussion. The way, he says, is through sympathy. 'It seems to me', he remarks—

that what happens, when an author creates a vital character, is a sort of give and take. The author may put into that character, besides its other attributes, some trait of his own, some strength or weakness, some tendency to violence or to indecision, some eccentricity even, that he has found in himself...Some bit of himself that the author gives to a character may be the germ from which the life of that character starts...I believe that the author imparts something of himself to his characters...[48]

In fact, the objectivity or 'absolute vision' that is felt to exist in drama is rather a matter of form and should not be ascribed to some absolute objective imagination. Whether writing lyric or drama, the poet is—he must be—subjective in varying degrees according to the poetic situation. His self-consciousness always imprints itself on his creations. In fact, since the dramatic poet enacts the situation or experience that is his subject, his involvement in it is much deeper and subtler than that of the lyric poet who usually aims at representing, not the process by which an experience is formed, but only the finished product. The dramatic poet brings in more facets of his personality and more complexes of his experience into his creation than the lyric poet.

IV

Though fundamentally the impulse behind all poetry is the same, drama is a special poetic mode[49] in more than one way. Drama, Ronald Peacock observes,

> can only emerge when the imagination functions in a quite special way, showing sympathy for all the innumerable and above all conflicting aspects of human character. For only then can it create the *dramatis personae* with interest and vividness, and lay the foundations for the dialectic of drama, in which people react on each other, with all the situations arising in consequence. Whatever is said about life, philosophy, religion, morals, man, or nature, whatever subtlety of spirit or feeling the poet proposes, has to be said in these terms.[50]

The dramatic vision of life is founded on a profound sense of human relationships and antagonisms expressed in sympathetic re-creation. Wordsworth has written of the 'human and dramatic Imagination' as against the 'enthusiastic and meditative Imagination'; and of the first the works of Shakespeare are cited as an inexhaustible source.[51] Imagination, in its dramatic mode, accepts the world of humanity as the primary object of its attention, and endeavours to see it and present it, not exactly, but steadily and as a whole. In order to do so, it seeks patiently for maturity, detachment, impersonality of judgement, an artistic method; that is, while it begins with the local and the concrete as its foundation, it actually goes beyond them. This imaginative mode displays itself as a responsive openness to life, a firm grasp on the centrally human, a respect for the present reality we all share, an allegiance to the objective, and a mistrust of abstraction from the total complexity of human experience. The dramatic mode of creation is thus one which presents complexities instead of abstractions, and in which the values are implicit and implied, though they may also find, as in the Elizabethan drama, direct expression—in 'overt statement of meanings.' It bases the statement of value in perception and gives the idea with its genesis, establishing its validity, which may conform to a public order of values, but is given as the experience of an identifiable person. This is what A.R. Thompson means when he says that drama works by 'implication' rather than by 'preachment'.[52]

But just saying that the dramatic mode of imagination is 'human', expressing itself in terms of human character, is not enough. This alone does not adequately bring out the unique character of the dramatic imagination. Both dramatic and lyrical poetry present virtual life as a self-contained form, a unit of experience in which every element is organically related to every other. Actual experience has no such closed form. Imagination gives it a form and a character and shapes it into a distinct unit, which can be further subjected to analysis and judgement. Everything actual must be transformed by imagination into something purely experiential: that is the fundamental principle of poetry.[53] But whereas poetry creates 'the illusion of life as a realm of events—completed, lived, as words formulate them—events that compose a Past,' drama presents the poetic illusion in a different way, not as finished realities or "events": immediate, visible responses of human beings make its semblance of life. Its basic abstraction is the act, which springs from the past, but is directed towards the future, and is always great with things to come.'[54] After distinguishing two types of poetry, 'narrative' and 'representative', Bacon in one of his illuminating perceptions defines the latter, that is drama, as 'a visible history...an image of actions as if they were present, as history is of actions in nature as they are, that is past.'[55]

In his discourse on "The Nature of Dramatic Illusion", Charles Morgan defines 'illusion' as the impregnating force in drama.[56] 'Illusion', he suggests, 'is form in suspense.'[57] The effect of drama is based on anticipation. We are not influenced by the form itself, the completed thing, but by our anticipations of completion. This 'suspense of form', by which is meant the 'incompleteness of a known completion', is to be distinguished from common suspense—the suspense of plot, which is but a structural accident. The 'suspense of form' is essential to the dramatic art.[58] The poignancy of drama comes 'not from any comparison with actuality, but from the fact that the two great realms of envisagement—past and future—intersect in the present, which consequently has not the pure imaginative form of either memory or prophecy, but a peculiar apprearance of its own which we designate as "immediacy" or "now".'[59] This tension between the past and the future is what gives to acts, situations, and even such constituent elements as gestures and attitudes and tones, in drama, the peculiar intensity known as dramatic quality.

Drama is an act (by which we may understand any sort of human response, physical or mental) or experience in making. This is not to say that drama is an exact representation of an actual experience; it is an art. As such, 'psychical distance' requires it, like other forms of art, to deal entirely in illusions. Delusions—even the quasi-delusion of make-belief—aims at the opposite effect, the greatest possible nearness. To seek delusion and the belief that drama is an exact portrayal of actual happenings is to deny that drama is art.[60] Drama, as poetry, is an abstraction and so a special kind of experience. It starts with a given situation and imposes a pattern upon the situation according to the poet's imaginative orientation. It selects and emphasises, whereas actual experience is a welter of sights, sounds, feelings, physical strains, expectations, and minute undeveloped reactions. Yet, because drama has to create the illusion of immediate experience, it includes, more than other forms of literature, the contrarieties of the total human experience. In order to make its semblance to life convincing it is incumbent on this kind of poetry to include in its texture the different threads of experience, though reforming and reordering them in the way of the imaginative transformation which is the basis of all arts. The dramatic mode of imagination is complex because it perceives from *within*, continually visualising new aspects of a given situation and its characters. It does not contemplate from the outside. A situation or a character perceived thus is not a static unit, but a growing thing. Here it may be profitable to dwell for a moment upon Bliss Perry's distinction of dramatic from lyrical poetry.[61] She describes Hamlet as a lyric poet, who could be 'lyrical' enough on occasions, but also 'retained the power of distinguishing between things as they actually were and things as they appeared to be in his weakness and his melancholy.'[62] The only sense in which we can accept the distinction is that the dramatic poet sees objects, which for him are human characters and situations, in the round, and therefore in all their complexity and with all their contradictions.

The present chapter has attempted to show the involutions

of the poetic process, both lyrical and dramatic, as well as the points of contact and difference between them. Arising from a common impulse, they are reincarnations in a symbolic form of the feeling of reality by which the artist achieves some sort of catharsis. In both the poet translates his perceptions into words by various devices, such as instinct, the example of his predecessors, and by a conscious effort to achieve the original imaginative pattern. Both require judicious combinations of the subjective and the objective; in both the unconscious creative impulse has to be checked and perfected by the conscious use of the poet's critical faculty. At the same time, while there is a generalised surface distinction between dramatic and lyrical poetry on the assumption that the one is more impersonal and objective than the other, drama, primarily concerned with human characters and their relationships and antagonisms, represents an experience in making which entails a wider and deeper involvement of the poet's personality and experience in his creation. Being a special kind of abstraction, the dramatic imagination evolves its own unique form, integrating the essentials of poetry with the essentials of drama in a subtilised manner and bringing the two inseparably together.

The imagination in its dramatic mode is a valid principle of artistic creation and would provide the essential approach in this study. The dramatic imagination finds expression in formal drama, but it may also manifest itself in poetry which is obviously lyrical. Many of Donne's poems not only emanate out of the poetic imagination, but are, in essence, drama, either in form or substance, or in both form and substance.

FOOTNOTES

1. G. Whalley, *Poetic Process*, London, 1953, p. 57.
2. Coleridge, *Biographia Literaria*, pp. 177-178, in *Coleridge-Biographia Literaria : Wordsworth—Prefaces and Essays on Poetry 1800-1815*, ed. G. Sampson, Cambridge, 1920.
3. Coleridge, *Lectures on Shakespeare 1811-1812*. Quoted in R.P. Cowl's *The Theory of Poetry in England*, London, 1914, p. 37.
4. *The Poetic Pattern*, London, 1956, p. 131. See also *Poetic Process*, p. 61.
5. *Scepticism and Poetry*, London, 1937, p. 23. The essential unsatisfactoriness of Kant's earlier stand has also been brought out in *Poetic Process*, pp. 56-61.
6. *English Critical Essays—Nineteenth Century*, ed. E.D. Jones, London, 1950, reprint, p. 355.
7. *Ibid.*, pp. 357-358.
8. See L.L. Whyte, "A Scientific View of The 'Creative Energy' of Man', *Aesthetics Today*, ed. M. Philipson, New York, 1961 p. 362. See also *Scepticism and Poetry*, pp. 21-22 ; *The Poetic Pattern*, p. 76.
9. *Poetic Process*, p. 61.
10. *Scepticism and Poetry*, p. 23. Also, L.E Gates, *Studies and Appreciations*, London, 1900, p. 215. According to Gates the shaping of a poem is 'all the time delicately controlled by the poet's conscious purpose and so growing intellectually significant...'
11. *Modern Poetry and the Tradition*, pp. 17-41.
12. *Ibid*, p. 24.
13. *Ibid*, pp. 24-25.
14. Wordsworth, Preface to the *Poems* of 1815, p. 206, in *Coleridge—Biographia Literaria : Wordsworth—Prefaces and Essays on Poetry 1800-1815*.
15. *Biographia Literaria*, pp. 57-58.
16. *Ibid.*, pp. 177-178.
17. *Ibid.*
18. See chapter on "Symbolic Extrication" in *Poetic Process*, pp. 104-115. D.G. James regards the poetic process, i.e. the secondary imagination, as a dissipation of the vague and distressing feeling of unrest and inner disturbance arising from the obscurity of primary perceptions—by a more adequate

self-consciousness. *Scepticism and Poetry*, pp. 112-113. This is the poetic 'catharsis'—'the liberation from his emotion which the poet must achieve and which makes his poetry' Robin Skelton (*The Poetic Pattern*, p. 179) and I.A. Richards (*Principles of Literary Criticism*, London, 1955, second ed., pp. 251-252) have described the poetic activity as an establishment, at a high and significant level, of 'psychic equilibrium and unified perceptiveness and of 'equilibrium of opposed impulses.' The establishment of such equilibrium is, I.A. Richards suspects, 'the ground-plan of the most valuable aesthetic responses.'

19. The term '*in* scape' is used here in the general sense of particularisation and not in the Thomistic or Scotist sense in relation to form and matter. G.M. Hopkins held the Scotist view and coined the term 'inscape'.

20. This reminds us of Kenneth Burke's view in *Philosophy of Literary Form : Studies in Symbolic Action*. New York, 1957, revised ed. abridged by the author : 'Critical and imaginative works are answers to questions posed by the situation in which they arose.' (p. 3) It is thus that poetry is 'symbolic action', with which the poet resolves a situation (p. 9). and the locus of the assertion is in the '*structural powers*' by which the poet encompasses the situation (p. 16).

21. "A Scientific View of the 'Creative Energy' of Man", pp. 361-362. ee also I.A. Richards, *Principles of Literary Criticism*, p. 29 : '...much that goes to produce a poem is, of course, unconscious.'

22. *Poetic Process*, p. 114.

23. *Scepticism and Poetry*, pp. 46-48 : Imagination is of momentous importance to the total life of personality. The task of embodying his imaginative experience in a wider imaginative pattern is for the poet 'a necessity of his experience...when it comes into strenuous life, as it does in the poet, It has its springs in a deeply felt need, the satisfaction of which becomes an increasing necessity to him.' This need is for a single grasp of prehension of life; the poet endeavours to build out of the fragments of his experience a unified perception of the whole of life. When the imagination withdraws itself from this conscious labour of creation into the contemplation of a world to the reality of which it is indifferent, and when it is exercised for its own sake, it deteriorates into fancy.

24. *The Poetic Pattern*, p. 180. See also L.L. Whyte, pp. 361-362.

25. T. S. Eliot, The Three Voices of Poetry'', *On Poetry and Poets*, London, 1957, second impression, pp. 97-98 : A lyric poet starts with an inert embryo or 'creative germ' ; on the other hand there is language, the resources of words at the poet's command. He must find words for what has been called the 'creative germ'.

26. *The Poetic Pattern*, p. 10.

27. *Poetic Process*, p. 114. See also L.C. Knights, "In search of Fundamental Values", *The Times Literary Supplement—The Critical Moment*, No. 3, 204, July 26, 1963, p. 569 : On looking for the point on which the edifice of criticism is raised, he finds it in 'the energy of mind and imagination released by the creative use of words.'

28. *Principles of Literary Criticism.* p. 29.

29. *The Common Asphodel*, Hamish Hamilton, 1949, p. 1.

30. *The Making of a Poem*, first published in *The Partisan Review*, summer 1946 ; included in *The Creative Process*, California, 1952, pp. 116-118.

31. C. D. Lewis, *The Poetic Image*, London, 1947, pp. 69, 71 ; *Poetic Process*, p. 114.

32. T.S. Eliot, *The Use of Poetry and the Use of Criticism*, London, 1933, p. 146 ; K. Burke, *Counter-Statement*, Chicago, 1957, second ed., pp. 53-55 ; Cleanth Brooks, *Modern Poetry and the Tradition*, p. 25.

33. *The Poetic Pattern*, p. 88.

34. *Table Talk*, April 20, 1833. Quoted in I.A. Richard's *Coleridge on Imagination*, London, 1950, second ed., p. 75.

35. *Coleridge on Imagination*, p. 97.

36. *Scepticism and Poetry*, pp. 115-116. I.A. Richards elaborates this with great insight and clarity in *Principles of Literary Criticism*, pp. 251-252 : 'The equilibrium of opposed impulses, which we suspect to be the ground-plan of the most valuable aesthetic responses, brings into play far more of our personality than is possible in experiences of a more defined emotion. We cease to be oriented in one definite direction ; more facets of the mind are exposed and, what is the same thing, more aspects of things are able to affect us. To respond, not through one narrow channel of interest, but simultaneously and coherently through many, is to be *disinterested* in the only sense of the word which concerns us here. A state of mind which is not disinterested is one which sees things only from one standpoint or under one aspect ...Of course without some interest we should not see them at all

but the less any one particular interest is indispensable, the more *detached* our attitude becomes. And to say that we are *impersonal* is merely a curious way of saying that our personality is more completely involved.'

37. *British Journal of Psychology*, June 1912, p. 91.
38. *The Encyclopaedia Britannica*, Cambridge, 1911, eleventh ed. vol. xxi, pp. 877-890.
39. *Ibid.*, p. 882.
40. *Ibid.*, p. 884.
41. *Ibid.*, p. 882.
42. *A Study of Poetry*, New York, 1920, pp. 228-235.
43. *Essays and Studies*, English Association, vol. xix, 1933, pp. 7-28. See also E.M.W. Tillyard's "The Personal Heresy in Criticism : A Rejoinder", *Essays and Studies*, English Association, vol. xx, 1934, pp. 7-20.
44. "The Personal Heresy in Criticism," p. 13.
45. "The Three Voices of Poetry", p. 100 : 'I think that in every poem, from the private meditation to the epic or the drama, there is more than one voice to be heard. If the author never spoke to himself, the result would not be poetry...But if the poem were exclusively for the author, it would be a poem in a private and unknown language.' See also C.S. Lewis's "The Personal Heresy in Criticism", p. 26.
46. "Poetry", p. 883.
47. *Biographia Literaria*, p. 64.
48. "The Three Voices of Poetry", pp. 93-94.
49. See Susanne K. Langer, *Feeling and Form*, London, 1953, p. 306. While accepting that the impulse behind all poetry is common, what he calls 'Gottfried Benn's unknown, dark *psychic material*' or 'the octopus or angel with which the poet struggles', T.S. Eliot says that between the three kinds of poetry to which the three voices correspond, there is 'a certain difference of process.' "The Three Voices of Poetry". pp. 100-101.
50. *The Art of Drama*, London, 1960, second impression with some corrections, p. 178.
51. Preface of 1815 in *Coleridge—Biographia Literaria: Wordsworth—Preface and Essays on Poetry 1800-1815*, pp. 213-214.
52. *The Anatomy of Drama*, California, 1946, p. 393.
53. *Feeling and Form*, p. 258. The substance of drama is an image of human life. 'It is a fabric of illusory experience, and that is the essential product of poesis.'

54. *Ibid.*, p. 306.

55. *Advancement of Learning,* 1605. Quoted in R.P. Cowl's *The Theory of Poetry in England,* pp. 157-158. According to F.B. Gummere, in *A Handbook of Poetics,* London, 1913, p. 58, drama unites the past and the present, the conditions of epic and lyric respectively, and gives us 'the past in the present.' Events are the basis of epic, but in drama they unroll themselves before our eyes.

56. "The Nature of Dramatic Illusion", *Essays by Divers Hands,* New Series, vol. xii, 1933, p. 67.

57. *Ibid.*, p. 70.

58. *Ibid.*, pp. 70-71.

59. *Feeling and Form,* p. 308.

60. " 'Psychical Distance' as a Factor in Art and an Aesthetic Principle ', p. 91.

61. *A Study of Poetry,* pp. 228-235.

62. *Ibid.*, pp. 235-236.

CHAPTER III

Satires

I

Donne's *Satires*, like most of his *Elegies*, were written before 1598-99.[1] The earliest date assignable to them is 1593. On the back of the Harlian MS. 5110 in the British Museum is inscribed :

"Jhon Dunne his Satires
 Anno Domini 1593"

Thus they belong to the period of that sudden outburst of formal satire and satirical comedy which distinguishes the last years of the sixteenth century. It was brought about by a number of deep currents of influence, including the disruptive social and economic changes of the time, which are reflected in the growth of an interest first in realism and then in psychology (in those days called 'anatomizing') in the early 1590s.[2] It shows itself, for instance, in Sir John Davies's indecent society epigrams published in 1593 as well as in his highly introspective *Nosce Teipsum* (1599). The change is best epitomised in Greene's *Groatsworth of Wit* (1592), which starts as a romance but ends as a piece of stark, disillusioned realism. The 1590s mark the first blossoming of satire in English literature. Formal satire flourished in the hands of Donne, Hall, Marston, among others, and there was Ben Jonson writing his satirical comedies. In this sudden outburst we perceive a reaction against most of the literary ideals and fashions which had hitherto prevailed; and a declaration, in so many words, that it was time to see things as they

56

really were. Spenser had envied the happiness of his paper
in being touched by the 'lily hands' of the lady who governed
his life; he was jealous of his lines because they would be
read in the starry light of her 'lamping eyes.' But when
Donne loses his mistress's bracelet, he regrets the loss, not
because the bracelet was the colour of her hair, nor because
it had touched her arm, nor because its links symbolised the
intertwining of their affections, but because it would cost
him a lot of money to replace. The occasion of the loss
gives him the excuse for arguing which woman is worth good
money. Here we have an instance of reaction against the
earlier romanticism and idealism: a disenchanted resolve to
be at all cost realistic, to see things as they are, and to
present them (as Jonson said) in 'language such as men do
use.'[3]

Donne made his intention clear in *Satire I* :

At birth, and death, our bodies naked are;
And till our Souls be unappareled
Of bodies, they from bliss are banished.
Man's first blest state was naked, when by sin
He lost that, yet he was cloth'd but in beasts' skin,
And in this coarse attire, which I now wear,
With God, and with the Muses I confer.
(11. 42-48)

These lines express Donne's choice of aim in his *Satires*. At
one level, their roughness of style may be regarded as just
an acceptance of a popular convention : of the current
popular notion, arising from the long persisting lexicographi-
cal error which confused the English 'satyre' with the Greek
satyros and ignored its connection with the Latin *satura*, that
satire should be loose-jointed, crudely devised, and obscurely
and harshly worded.[4] But at another level there is a possibility that it resulted from the dictates of his own temper.[5]

In that case a significant aspect of Donne's *Satires* would be their projection of his personality and their unmistakable individuality of tone. May I submit that in the *Satires* we move together with Donne, who sometimes addresses us directly, sometimes meditates by himself, and sometimes enacts characters and situations in the manner of drama, through the Court, the law courts, and the streets of London.

II

Hallet Smith does not approve a formal approach to the Elizabethan satire for two reasons.[6] Firstly, the question of form is a difficult one in dealing with any kind of poetry in the sixteenth century. Secondly, only 'a smug and complacent society' (that of Pope, for instance), as the Elizabethan society was not, could 'departmentalise its experience so much that it finds an adequate separate form for its satire.' 'The Elizabethans', Hallet Smith ovserves, 'saw the satirical in the shadow of the pastoral, in the obverse of the heroic, in the extravagance of love poetry.' It ought to be noticed that in his love lyrics Donne borrows many of the tricks and much of the material formerly reserved for satire and thus innovates the lyric to a remarkable degree, extending it to cover a wider and subtler range of experience as well as expression. The style of a good half of the *Elegies* and of some of the *Songs and Sonnets* is close to that of satirical poetry. The fourteenth *Elegy, A Tale of a Citizen and his Wife,* has a style similar to that of Horace's *Sermons* or conversation pieces; it is a kind of satirical verse-letter, but addressed to no one in particular, recounting the sort of incident that would make a funny story in a tavern. Some of the *Elegies*, even though they go deeper emotionally and strike us with greater force, are still on the level of satire. Furthermore, the models, the sources, from which the Elizabethan satirists could draw their conventions, were mixed. Just as Spenser at the same time tried to follow both Chaucer and the humanist pastoral writers, the Elizabethan writers of verse satire had not only Juvenal and Persius to imitate, but also Horace and the author of *Piers Ploughman*. It is significant that Donne's first religious poem, *Satire III*, is not a divine poem but a satire.

Mary Randolph, on the other hand, favours a formal approach to the Elizabethan verse satire.[8] She finds in the genre a 'specific vertebrate form or architectural design despite its apparently loose-meshed, casually discursive surface.'[9] And it may be argued, without in any way coutradicting, either the mercurial fluidity and elusiveness of the satirical spirit by which it flows into and fuses itself with other essentially or even temporarily congenial forms, or the claim that the significant sources of satire are not literary or philosophical but social and economic,[10] that the approach suggested by Mary Randolph is more helpful to purposes of literary appreciation.

Mary Randolph traces the 'form' of the formal verse satire to the satires of Lucilius, Horace, Persius, and Juvenal; and the formal satire, appearing in England during the last decade of the sixteenth century, was based on the classical model.[11] The introduction was perfectly natural. Besides there being familiarity with a certain amount of theory of satire derived from the classics and from Italian critics of the Renaissance, the classical satirists had been for a long time in the Latin curriculum of the English grammar school. If the Renaissance English satirist thought at all critically of form in connection with verse satire, he left no printed expression of his thought. But, as Mary Randolph has pointed out, 'certain elementary points in connection with the satires of Horace, Persius, and Juvenal were immediately visible to him; indeed, he could hardly escape them.'[12] 'From observation and study of the classical satires, then, the English Renaissance satirists learned these elementary things about form: that Satires were usually written in clusters of indeterminate number,...that their lengths were extremely variable; and that they were semi-dramatic and monometric.'[13] Donne wrote a cluster of five satires; Lodge, four; Hall, thirtyfive—the largest collection of satires at his time; and Marston, eleven. As far as the length of satires is concerned, although the first, second, third, and fifth satires of Donne are almost of equal length (112, 112, 110, and 91 lines respectively), the fourth satire (244 lines) is more than double the length of the other satires.

III

On examining Donne's *Satire I* we see that it has exactly that 'specific vertebrate form or architectural design' which Mary Randolph finds in the formal verse satire. It is bipartite in structure. There are two clearly distinguishable parts. While in the one a specific vice is turned about on all its sides and thoroughly exposed, its opposing virtue is recommended in the other. The satire attacks a 'fondling motley humorist' as also his adored ostentatious figures who frequented London streets at the time of Donne. The value against which the 'humorist' and the other figures are observed is that of the austere life of a scholar (11. 1-10), of simplicity and nakedness (11. 37-48).

The entire piece is enclosed in an outer shell-like framework. The 'combative hollow man or Interlocutor' or 'Adversarius', serving as a 'whip and spur' to the satirist, is that same 'humorist.' The 'Adversarius' ever draws out from the satirist, by his words and actions, fresh comment and anecdote concerning the vice in question. A panoramic background of a London street is lightly but clearly sketched. Altogether, then, we have the minimum essentials of the quasi-dramatic genre that the formal verse satire is: two actors or participants, the satirist and his 'Adversarius'; a setting of some kind; and a thesis to be advanced. *Satire I* presents a situation in which the poet was persuaded to

60

leave his books and take a walk with an absurdly foppish man who, after smiling at 'every fine silken painted fool' they came across, left him, first for a celebrated tobacco-smoker, then for a celebrated judge of clothes, and finally for his mistress in whose house he quarrelled with other gallants and was turned out of doors with a fractured head.

Within this outer quasi-dramatic framework lies the satire itself wherein the irrational and foolish court paid by the 'humorist' to every ostentatious man is, as it were, turned about on a pivot and its various sides and facets are mercilessly exposed and illumined by a wide variety of lively exegetical devices. The satirist is apprehensive that his foppish friend will leave him in the middle of the street for the very first 'spruce' fellow that comes along and so asks him to promise :

> Thou wilt not leave me in the middle street,
> Though some more spruce companion thou dost meet,
> Not though a captain do come in thy way
> Bright partial guilt, with forty dead men's pay,
> Not though a brisk perfum'd piert Courtier
> Deigns with a nod, thy courtesy to answer.
> Nor come a velvet Justice with a long
> Great train of blue coats, twelve, or fourteen strong,
> Wilt thou grin or fawn on him, or prepare
> A speech to court his beauteous son and heir !
>
> (11. 15-24)

This is followed by a more direct account of the fop's vice :

> Oh Monstrous, superstitious puritan,
> Of refin'd manners, yet ceremonial man,
> That when thou meet's one, with inquiring eyes
> Dost search, and like a needy broker prize

The silk, and gold he wears, and to that rate
So high or low, dost raise thy formal hat:
That will consort none, until thou have known
What lands he hath in hope, or of his own,
As though all thy companions should make thee
Jointures, and marry thy dear company.

(11. 27-36)

The irrationalities of the 'humorist' are brought out by means of some clever analogies in lines 53-64. However, his follies are most vividly portrayed in the second half of the satire, partly by description (11. 67-82), but mainly through action and dialogue, most elaborately and meticulously done and sustained in an astonishingly organic unity of the essentials of drama and poetry. The rarity and the fineness of this combination are visible in every line of the following excerpt from the poem :

Now leaps he upright, jogs me, & cries, Do you see
Yonder well favoured youth?   which? Oh, 'tis he
That dances so divinely; Oh, said I,
Stand still, must you dance here for company?
He droop'd, we went, till one (which did excel
Th' Indians, in drinking Tobacco well)
Met us; they talk'd; I whispered, let 'us go,
'T may be you smell him not, truly I do;
He hears not me, but, on the other side
A many-coloured Peacock having spied,
Leaves him and me; I for my lost sheep stay;
He follows, overtakes, goes on the way,
Saying, him who I last left, all repute
For his device, in hansoming a suit,
To judge of lace, pink, panes, print, cut, and plight,
Of all the Court, to have the best conceit;
Our dull Comedians want him, let him go;

But oh, God strengthen thee, why stoop'st thou so ?
Why? he hath travelled; Long ? Know; but to me
(Which understand none) he doth seem to be
Perfect French, and Italian; I replied,
So is the Pox; He answered not, but spi'd
More men of sort, of parts, and qualities;
At last his Love he in a window spies,
And like light dew exhal'd, he flings from me
Violently ravish'd to his lechery
Many were there, he could command no more;
He quarrell'd fought, bled; and turn'd out of door
    Directly came to me hanging the head,
    And constantly a while must keep his bed.

(11. 83-112)

The conversation begins abruptly and continues eliptically, broken and interrupted here and there, throughout the whole elaborate, studied rhetorical apparatus. Here it would be useful to remember that classical satire, as it was descended from oral genres, was still in Augustan Rome designed to be recited in public arcade or forum and was probably energetically dramatised as the speaker gave his lines.[14]

To illustrate his thesis, win his case, and move his audience to thought and perhaps to psychological action, Donne utilises miniature dramas such as we have seen in lines 83-90 and 100-104. He also uses sententious proverbs: 'Here are God's conduits, grave Divines; and here/Nature's Secretary, the Philosopher.' (11. 5-6); quotable maxims :

'Why should'st thou.../Hate virtue, though she be naked, and bare?' (11. 37-41); brief seirors (11. 37-48); sharp debates; series of vignettes; swiftly sketched but painstakingly built up satirical characters such as those of the captain, the courtier and the justice in lines 16-22; apostrophes and invocations to abstractions—in brief, anything and every thing to push his argument forward to its philosophical and psychological conclusion in much the same manner as events might push action to denouement in drama.

With great care the poet governs point, compactness, speed, climax, contrast, surprise, and a score more of the special effects so well illustrated by the best in Shakespeare and equally necessary for good and effective satire. Holding these varied materials together internally is the unifying thesis or core of argument, while the outer frame serves as external enclosure for the entire piece. Thus, whatever simplicity and nonchalance this satire seems to have is only an assumed simplicity of verbal surface beneath which there exists a skilfully evolved and delicately managed development of dialectical argument in a dramatic pattern. The same quasi-dramatic structure, though in a lesser degree, is found in the other four satires too.

The sins of lawyers form the subject of *Satire II*. It is addressed to 'Sir' (whatever his identity is, he is undoubtedly a *dramtis persona*). The 'bold soul' of line 63, addressed and invoked to esteem aright such worthless people as those 'which choose/Law practice for mere gain' (11. 62-63), is the 'Sir' or the type character to whom the whole poem is addressed.[15] The 'Adversarius', very different from the 'humorist' of *Satire I*, is just a shadow, only a mute decoy who listens to the satirist's invectives against the lawyer poet Coscus (the anonymous author of the sonnet sequence *Zepheria*), and then after a sudden transition at lines 61-62, against those who choose the profession of law for mere gain. As such *Satire II* does not have a situation like *Satire I*. There is, for all practical purposes, only one participant, and there is also no setting of any sort. There is only a thesis to be argued and the satirist expounds it from the first to the last. The manner is discursive, anecdotal, and elusive: concrete examples, presented with the maximum of colourful and realistic detail, mingle with passages of generalisation, but the ebullience and liveliness of *Satire I* are missing. This is only to say that Donne's satires are very uneven. In the present satire we are often taken by a fine and just observation, a clever example, a momorable phrase, but the entire thing is so abstract and wanting in dramatic unity that one is tempted to agree with K.W. Gransden's remark that 'one suddenly finds one has lost the thread of the often difficult argument, and is becoming bored.'[16]

Satire II is 'much less individual and characteristic.'[17] The poem opens with a generalisation:

> Sir, though (I thank God for it) I do hate
> Perfectly all this town, yet there's one state
> In all ill things so excellently best,
> That hate, towards them, breeds pity towards the rest.
>
> (11. 1-4)

This is followed by an account of the sins of poetry which, 'like the Pestilence and old fashion'd love', catch men 'Riddlingly' and cannot be removed 'till it be starv'd out' (11. 5-9). Some poets there are who labour over scenes (starving themselves in the process) for 'idiot actors' (11. 11-16), Others would 'move Love by rhythms', but magic is now, the satirist says, ineffective, and 'Pistolets are the best Artillery' (11. 17-20). Then there are poets who 'write to Lords, rewards to get' (11. 21-22). But—

> ...he is worse, who (beggarly) doth chaw
> Others' wit's fruits, and in his ravenous maw
> Rankly digested, doth those things out-spew,
> As his own things; and they are his own, 'tis true,
> For if one eat my meat, though it be known
> The meat was mine, th' excrement is his own:
>
> (11. 25-30)

But these, the poet declares, like other monstrous sinners

such as lechers, usurers, drunkards, swearers, do not harm
him. They only punish themselves. What the satirist cannot
stand, however, is Coscus—

> Whom time (which rots all, and makes botches pox,
> And plodding on, must make a calf an ox)
> Hath made a Lawyer, which was (alas) of late
> But a scarce Poet;...
>
> (11. 41-44)

It is with relation to Coscus that the irony of the 'so
excellently best' of line 3 is clarified. A sort of parody-drama
of Coscus' verse alongwith the satirist's comments is given in
lines 44-60 and makes an amusing reading:

> ...jollier of this state,
> Then are new benefic'd ministers, he throws
> Like nets, or lime-twigs, wheresoever he goes,
> His title of Barrister, on every wench,
> And wooes in language of the Pleas, and Bench:
> A motion, Lady; speak Coscus; I have been
> In love, ever since *tricesimo* of the Queen,
> Continual claims I have made, injunctions got
> To stay my rival's suit, that he should not
> Proceed; spare me; In Hillary term I went,
> You said, if I return'd next size in Lent,
> I should be in remitter of your grace;
> In th' interim my letters should take place
> Of affidavits: words, words, which would tear
> The tender labyrinth of a soft maid's ear,
> More, more, than ten Sclavonians scolding, more
> Than when winds in our ruin'd Abbeys roar.

Then by a very abrupt and obscure transition (11. 61-62)
Donne proceeds to satirise the man who takes up the practice

of law for mere gain and ensures for himself a reputation worse than that of 'imbrothel'd strumpets prostitute' (11. 65-76). The avarice of the lawyer comes in for special attention and there is exhaustive and contemptuous detail in the simile in lines 81-86 reminiscent of Ben Jonson's practice:

> For as a thrifty wench scraps kitching-stuff,
> And barrelling the droppings, and the snuff,
> Of wasting candles, which in thirty year
> (Relique-like kept) perchance buys wedding gear;
> Piecemeal he gets lands, and spends as much time
> Wringing each Acre, as men pulling prime;...

There is large exuberance in the following backhanded satire on the reformed churches (11. 87-96). Finally, the standpoint of the satirist, that of an upholder of the old-fashioned virtue against a degenerating mankind, is given (11. 103-112).

Satire III is similar to *Satire II* in so far as the 'Adversarius' is here, too, just a mute listener to the poet. The satire is aimed against those who refuse to make the effort to find truth in religion, or make the search wrongly on narrow sectarian lines. The positive point towards which the whole exegetical and rhetorical procedure is aimed is that the Elizabethan courage which found expression in war, commercial traffic, and discoveries, in a bold defiance of the dangers of unknown lands and distant shores, and in stout maintenance of honour in duels, should be devoted to the greatest venture of all and the most significant—that search for truth which would determine the real future, not the fading, short-lived future of the world.

In fact, *Satire III* is not a satire in the ordinary sense. It is rather an epistle on the subject of finding the true religion. Grierson has indicated the similarity between this satire and the opening as well as closing stanzas of *The Progress of the Soul*. Both are, by tone and temper, connected with Donne's verse-letters and in both the personal interest is very marked. 'Each is', Grierson says, 'a vivid picture of the inner working of Donne's soul at a critical period in his life.'[18] In the third satire, Donne is inspired by a subject that affected him, perhaps, more vitally than the subjects of his other satires. It contains wit, seen in the imagery which is largely sexual, but the wit is transformed by a genuine passion and an eager mind at work, the last of which makes the poem intensely dramatic. We feel the conceits coming from a man whose participation in what he is saying is not only cerebral but also emotional. There is an undoubted feeling of sincerity in the poem and its rough lines are penetrated by an intense hunger for truth.

Most of the poem is surprisingly, we discover, an extended sexual conceit, and the poem affects us through this. Underlying the satire is a picture of the amorous proclivities of the Elizabethan gallant:

Is not our Mistress fair Religion,
As worthy of all our Souls' devotion,
As virtue was to the first blinded age?
Are not heaven's joys as valiant to assuage
Lusts, as earth's honour was to them?

(11. 5-9)

Here we have the same combination of the divine and the carnal loves which is found in many of Donne's divine poems:

Take me to you, imprison me, for I
Except you' enthral me, never shall be free,
Nor ever chaste, except you ravish me.

(*Holy Sonnet XIV*, 11. 12-14)

Betray kind husband thy spouse to our sights,
And let mine amorous soul court thy mild Dove,
Who is most true, and pleasing to thee, then
When she' is embrac'd and open to most men.

(*Holy Sonnet XVIII*, ll. 11-14)

About religious intolerance, the poet says:

...and must every he
Which cries not, Goddess, to thy Mistress, draw,
Or eat thy poisonous words? courage of straw !

(ll. 26-28)

For the current love of the world Donne chooses the metaphor:

So the world's self, thy other lov'd foe, is
In her decrepit wane, and thou loving this,
Dost love a withered and worn strumpet;....

(ll. 37-39)

For the various sects of religion Donne presents characters, surprisingly individualised, who have eccentric and stubborn preferences. Mirreus, the Catholic, 'Thinking her unhous'd here, and fled from us,' seeks her at Rome because he knows that she was there a thousand years ago and he loves her rags so. Crantz, the Puritan, loves nought but her who at Geneva is known as religion, 'plain, simple, sullen, young,/Contemptuous, yet unhandsome' as some lecherous men find no wenches wholesome but 'coarse country drudges.' There is evidence elsewhere that Donne loved neither of these extremes. In that brilliantly witty piece, *The Will*, he jibes at both:

My faith I give to Roman Catholics;
All my good works unto the Schismatics
Of Amsterdam;...

(ll. 19-21)

Graius, the Anglican, will take only that religion which is handed him by his governors, like those that marry solely by the decision of their guardians. The careless Phrygius abhors all religions, like a man who, knowing some women whores, dares marry none. His opposite, Graccus, finds no essential difference between them and loves them all alike, promiscuously.

If this is wit, we do not feel it. Rather it is the instrument with which the poet makes vivid what we have referred to as an eager mind at work; the mind of the poet desperately trying to get out of a dilemma like the protagonist of a play in conflict. Many of Donne's poems emanate out of the imagination and are, in essence, drama, in either form or substance or both. *Satire III* is an instance of drama in subtance; *Satire I* of drama in form.

Satire IV like the first, deals with a bore. Donne has based this satire on Horace's *Ibam forte via Sacra*, but follows a quite independent line, recreating a conventional scene with a new force. Horace's theme is at bottom a contrast between his friendship with Maecenas and 'the way in which vulgar and pushing people sought, and sought in vain, to obtain an introduction.' Donne, like Horace, describes a bore, but makes this the occasion for a general picture of the hangers-on at Court. The vein is far less serious than that in which the third satire is written, yet it probably bears the impress of personal feeling. When Donne came to write this satire, in his early twenties, it is quite possible that he himself had been angling for a minor post at the Court. But the influence of the Catholic Church—possibly through his mother —was at work. His mother was of high lineage, a direct descendent of Sir Thomas More's sister. It is probable that she dwelt much on this ancestry. The fourth satire shows how it was with the poet who, with the memory of a position rightly his, saw it snatched away by inglorious parvenus in an age of shifting social values. The fierce contempt for

Elizabeth's courtiers in the satire may be regarded as Donne's
apologia to himself for failure in a contest in which he had
never really put his heart:

> ...Thou which since yesterday hast been
> Almost about the whole world, hast thou seen,
> O Sun. in all thy journey, Vanity,
> Such as swells the bladder of our Court? I
> Think he which made your waxen garden, and
> Transported it from Italy to stand
> With us, at London, flouts our presence, for
> Just such gay painted things, which no sap, nor
> Taste have in them, ours are; And natural
> Some of the stocks are, their fruits, bastard all.

(11. 165-174)

Such, as Donne saw them, were the courtiers of Elizabeth. Donne's mother, like most single-hearted Catholics of
the time, must have regarded this lady as an upstart Jezebel,
who unjustly claimed power from God instead of submitting
to His will. R.S. Hillyer reads an interesting double meaning
in a reference in *Satire III*:

> Is not our Mistress fair Religion,
> As worthy of all our Souls' devotion,
> As virtue was to the first blinded age?

In writing these lines, Hillyer says, 'Donne was not thinking
merely of theology...Such phrasing smacks too much of
courtly eulogy to escape notice as an ironic twisting of it.
The last decade of the reign was astir with double meanings...
Donne was not entirely blind to the possibilities of his
training.'[19]

The verse of *Satire IV* is more explicitly dramatic than that
of *Satire III*. It presents the situation of the poet going to

Court, being pestered by a courtier, and finally going back home to reflect on the folly and futility of those whom he has seen at Court. The poet, as he has put it, has the bad luck to go to Court, where he is at once accosted by a courtier—'Stranger than seven Antiquaries' studies,/Than Afric's Monsters, Guinea's rarities,' who pretends to be a great traveller, linguist, and repository of secrets. When this person names the poet and comes to him, the poor victim can only shudder and groan:

> I whisper, Go !
> How have I sinn'd, that thy wrath's furious rod,
> This fellow chooseth me?
>
> (11. 49-51)

This is followed by a long dialogue between the poet and the courtier, in the course of which the courtier reveals himself and the satirist (though apparently tortured and sweating) has some fun at the cost his adversary. Most of it is too overloaded with details to be appreciated, but parts of the dialogue are extremely lively and brilliant in their movement and pauses:

> He smack'd and cri'd, He's base, Mechanic, coarse,
> So are all your Englishmen in their discourse.
> Are not your Frenchmen neat? Mine? As you see,
> I have but one Frenchman, look, he follows me.
> Certes they are neatly cloth'd;—I, of this mind am,
> Your only wearing is your Grogaram.
> Not so Sir, I have more.
>
> (11. 81-87)

The joke first turns on the poet's pretending to misunderstand the bore's colloquial, but rather affected, indefinite use of 'your.' The poet applies it to himself and thus secures the initiative to deflate the vanity-swollen 'bladder' of the courtier. After saying 'Certes they [i.e. Frenchmen] are neatly cloth'd,' he rejoins: 'I, of this mind am,/Your only wearing is your Grogaram.' A similar example of humour arising out of confusion about a word (i e. 'spare') is found in lines 140-144:

> ...But the' hour
> Of mercy now was come; He tries to bring
> Me to pay a fine to 'scape his torturing,
> And says, Sir, can you spare me; I said, willingly;
> Nay, Sir, can you spare me a crown?

We may only conjecture what Donne could have achieved by continuing in such a comic vein. But this was not to be; detail is piled on detail. However, individual lines, here and there, are striking:

> And unto her protests, protests, protests,
> So much as at Rome would serve to have thrown
> Ten Cardinals into the Inquisition;
> And whispered by Jesu, so often, that a
> Pursevant would have ravish'd him away
> For saying of our Lady's psalter.

(11. 212-217)

Despite their texture, the lines do not add up to a structural whole. Dramatic elements such as situation, character and dialogue are lost in the crowd of detail and there is no clear plan or dominant idea as we have found in *Satire I*.

Satire V, dealing exclusively with officers and courts of law and suitors as well as the wrongs they do, broadens out into generality and condemns the satirist's age beyond measure. In *Satire I*, Donne ridicules only the superficial fool who takes seriously such tokens as costume. The sins of lawyers form the subject of *Satire II. Satire III* is aimed against those who refuse to make the effort to find truth in religion, or who make the search with a narrow mind. *Satire IV* attacks the courtiers of Elizabeth. In the first, second, and fourth satires, the poet's anger is constantly relieved by a sense of humour—by a comic perception of incongruity apart from the darker points in the objects of satire. On the other hand, the very opening of *Satire V* promises that there is going to be no laughter in it:

Thou shalt not laugh in this leaf, Muse, nor they
Whom any pity warms;...

(11. 1-2)

The poet reaffirms his intention of being humourless and remorseless in his attack against officers and courts of law and suitors:

What is he
Who Officers' rage, and Suitors' misery
Can write, and jest?

(11. 7-9)

There was hardly any set-back in the life of Donne at the time when *Satire V* was probably composed, so far as we know, which could justify the sombre change. However, a clue is provided by Grierson's account of the composition of this satire.[20] According to him, the words 'You Sir, whose righteousness she loves', etc. show that the poem was written after Donne had entered Sir Thomas Egerton's service, i.e. between 1598, if not earlier, and February 1601-2 when he was dismissed. The poem was probably written in 1598-99. Grierson finds in *Satire V* a note of enthusiasm as of one who has just entered on a service of which he is highly proud. The occasion of the poem was probably Egerton's endeavour to curtail the fees claimed by the Clerk of the Star Chamber. The enthusiasm of a young man, then, newly entered on service—his eagerness to impress his master with the didactic power of his pen, was perhaps at the root of the general and unmitigated condemnation of the satirist's own age that we fined in *Satire V*. This enthusiasm led the poet to adopt the mood of the 'malcontent' that was so fashionable then. There is nothing in the satire by which we may take it as an illustration of the habitual pessimism that is sometimes attributed to Donne. When he says:

> O Age of rusty iron! Some better wit
> Call it some worse name, if ought equal it;
> The iron Age *that* was, when justice was solid; now
> Injustice is sold dearer far...
>
> (11. 35-38)

he is not expressing a genuine pessimism but only appearing as a poseur, taking up an attitude of moral and intellectual superiority—the conventional pose of the satirist, and overdoing it. This may be the reason, if we accept Grierson's point, why the fifth satire is, among all the satires of Donne, the most unconvincing. It seems that Donne is here interested less in the things he is satirising and more in exhibiting how well he can argue and spin off conceits.

Beginning his argument in the poem with a syllogism—

> If all things be in all,
> As I think, since all, which were, are, and shall
> Be, be made of the same elements:
> Each thing, each thing implies or represents...,
>
> (11. 9-12)

Donne grants full licence to his fancy to arrive at whatever conclusions it may:

Then man is a world; in which, Officers
Are the vast ravishing seas; and Suitors,
Springs; now full, now shallow, now dry; which, to
That which drowns them, run: These self reasons do
Prove the world a man, in which, Officers
Are the devouring stomach, and Suitors
The excrements, which they void.

(11. 13-19)

This is followed by an antithetical use of couplets and
sustained conceits. In the passage which follows, the whole
point turns on the exploitation of the double meaning of the
word 'Angels' (spirits and coins): 'Judges are Gods; he
who made and said them so,/Meant not that men should be
forc'd to them to go,/By means of Angels.' However, the
most surprising invention is yet to come. 'fair laws', the poet
says, 'is established/Recorder to Destiny…and she/Speaks
Fate's words',

...but yet hath foul long nails,
With which she scracheth Suitors; In bodies
Of men, so in law, nails are th' extremities,
So Officers stretch to more than law can do,
As our nails reach what no else part comes to.

(11. 74-78)

Here, if anywhere, wit is an end in itself. The satire remains
just a collection of clever statements and we fail to see any
personality behind them—involved at more than the level of
intellect and ingenuity.

Taking all of Donne's five satires together, apart from
the poet's awareness of the literary kind he had adopted in
them,[21] their more or less common manner, harsh, discursive,
anecdotal, and allusive, and their mingling of concrete
examples—presented with the maximum of contemptuous and

realistic detail—with generalisation, a very significant aspect
is their projection of the poet's personality from the start and
their unmistakable individuality of tone. They are related
directly to the circumstances of his own career and are
reflections of his preoccupations with his own intellectual,
social, and spiritual progress. This distinguishes Donne as a
satirist from the other Renaissance satirists.[22] But even
more than this quality, it is the dramatised action in Donne's
satires, composed in nervous and frenetic images, which
sets them apart from other contemporary satires. Many
qualities of Donne's satires are also found in the works of
other Renaissance satirists. Davies's *In Ciprium*[23] draws a
character similar to the ostentatious fop in Donne's *Satire I*.
But whereas the scenes and events of Donne's satires at their
best are charcterised by passion and strength and every
character is depicted through action, Davies composes his
work in a still-life study. Hall's *Virgidemiarum*, written at
about the same time as Donne's satires,[24] exhibits an
experience of a wholly bookish kind unlike Donne's satires
which embody a dramatic vision of things and possess the
breath of life itself. The difference may be seen clearly if we
place side by side Donne's dramatisation (though in the vein
of parody) in *Satire II*, of Coscus' composition of verse in the
language of law (11.49-57), and Hall's satirical representation
of a type of literary affectation in the sixth satire of
Virgidemiarum :

> Another scorns the homespun thread of rhymes
> Matched with the lofty feet of elder times.
> Give me the numbered verse that Virgil sung
> And Virgil self shall speak the English tongue :
> Manhood and garboils shall he chant, with changed feet,
> And headstrong dactyls making music meet;
> The nimble dactyls striving to outgo
> The drawling spondees pacing it below;

The ling'ring spondees, labouring to delay
The breathless dactyls with a sudden stay.
Whoever saw a colt, wanton and wild,
Yoked with a slow-foot ox on fallow field,
Can right areed how handsomely besets
Dull spondees with the English dactylets.
If Jove speak English in a thund'ring cloud,
Thwick thwack, and riff raff, roars he out aloud.[25]

The extreme unevenness of Donne's satires cannot be, however, minimised or ignored. The first, second, and fourth satires are perceptibly and significantly dramatic. They have all an outer dramatic framework within which the satire itself is enclosed. However, there are differences which should be noted. Whereas the first and fourth satires provide perfect examples of the quasi-dramatic structure of the formal verse satire: they have two active participants, the satirist and an 'Adversarius', a background of some sort, and a thesis to be elaborated; the second satire has an 'Adversarius' who is a mere shadow, just a mute listener to the satirist, and no background. In spite of its perfect quasi-dramatic structure, the fourth satire is so overlarded with detail that no clear plan or dominant idea comes out of it as in the first and third satires. But all the three satires, namely, the first, second and fourth, employ dialogue, situation, and character in some marked form to illustrate their points, win their cases, and persuade their audience. A saving grace of all the three satires is the poet's sense of humour which constantly lightens his anger and refines the crudities. The fifth satire is grim and humourless, and we miss in it the fine dissolution of anger in humour. The poetry too suffers because of the relative absence of detachment on the part of the poet.

The quasi-dramatic architectural design followed by Donne in his satires can be found in the works of other

Renaissance satirists. What requires emphasising is that Donne went beyond just form and organisation. In his satires he goes deeper and is rooted in his vision of the life, the people, and the behaviour of his time. The sheer joy he manifests in the creation of character and the portrayal of human relationships, though only occasionally in the satires, goes beyond the limited end of the satirical form and is a sign of the presence of dramatic imagination functioning through profound sympathy with diverse conflicting aspects of human nature. The dramatic form in which this interest reveals itself produces the dialectic of drama in which people react on each other, with all the consequent results. The humorist of *Satire I*, Coscus 'a Lawyer, which was (alas) of late/But a scarce Poet'—of *Satire II*, and the courtier—'in immaculate clothes, and symmetry' Perfect as circles'—of *Satire IV* are not merely there to serve as 'whip and spur' to the satirist but truly dramatic creations. At the same time the characters in these satires, the satirist himself, the adversaries, and other satirical portraits are all embodiments of ideas and attitudes, and the dramatic situations in which these characters interact are at bottom a clash between ideas and attitudes and a dramatisation of Donne's vision of the social reality of his time fragmented in the satires for dramatic ends.

The poet's dependence on explicit systems of values, his expression of abstract norms by which he judges things, are a necessity of the genre he has adopted in his satires. But the importance of the parts which work by 'implication' cannot be overstated. Donne's satires come alive even today, when we are no longer interested in the physical or moral conditions of the last years of the sixteenth century, partly by their ingenious argument or by their occasional just observation, clever example, and memorable phrase, but mainly by those passages where the poet is at once sympathetic in the way of drama and disinterested in the way of all art. When this is wanting, all that the serious intentions of Donne can produce is only poor poetry as in *Satire V*. This satire is inadequate in its transformation of the actual into the experiential and so inadequate as poetry. It also fails as drama, because it does not give the sense, found in the whole of *Satire III* and in parts of the other three satires, of the immediate visible responses of human beings which is the basic abstraction of drama. Whenever Donne's poetry succeeds, it is for him not merely a question of literary devices but of an irresistible interest in human character and in the totality of human experience. When the dramatic vision fails, there is a descent to the mere intellectual or bathetic as in *Satire V*.

FOOTNOTES:

1. *Donne's Poetical Works*, vol. ii, 100-105.
2. T. Spencer, "Donne and His Age", *A Garland for John Donne*, pp. 180-183. In chapters i and ii of his *Shakespeare and the Nature of Man*, New York, 1942, he has illuminated the dilemma of the view of man as it produced tragedy, showing how the sceptical tradition represented by Montaigne viewed man as another animal and challenged the Platonic-humanistic glorification of man. The same dramatic contrast, he recognises, produces satire, although for satire the observation of social life and behaviour is probably more important than the sceptical theory. See also Hallet Smith, *Elizabethan Poetry*, Cambridge : Masachusetts, 1952, pp. 206-207 ; E.K. Chambers, "The Disenchantment of the Elizabethans", *Sir Thomas Wyatt and Collected Studies*, London, 1933.
3. Prologue to *Every Man in His Humour*.
4. Horace's theory of satire hand marked influence in Elizabethan England, both directly and indirectly. The critical doctrine of satire in *De Poeta* of Minturno adds to Horace's theory a principle which was important for the development of Renaissance satire.

As infirmities and wounds are the concern of medicine, Minturno says, so the passions and troubles of the mind are the concern of satire. You cure one with bitter medicines, the other with harsh words. This conception of satire was behind almost all the satires of the Renaissance. We see this in Shakespeare's Jaques when he proposes to set himself up as a satirist : cf. *As You Like It*, II, vii, 11.58-61. See also Hallet Smith, p. 219 ; Hugh Walker, *English Satire and Satirists*, Delhi, pp. 68-72.

5. Bernard Harris, *Elizabethan Poetry*, London, 1960, p. 191.

6. Hallet Smith, p. 207.

7. *Ibid.*

8. "The Structural Design of the Formal Verse Satire", *Philological Quarterly*, vol. xxi, 1942, pp. 368-384.

9. *Ibid.*, p. 368.

10. Hallet Smith, p. 194.

11. *Ibid.*, pp. 216-221.

12. Mary Randolph, p. 378. Also, pp. 378-380.

13. *Ibid.*, pp. 379-380.

14. *Ibid.*, p. 379 : 'Classical tradition had taught Ranaissance English satirists that formal satire was in direct descent from the old comedy and from the Greek Satyr-play and should therefore be quasi-dramatic in character.'

15. *Donne's Poetical Works*, vol. ii, p. iii.

16. *John Donne*, London, 1954, p. 102.

17. *The Monarch of Wit*, p. 110.

18. *Donne's Poetical Works*, vol. ii, p. xv.

19. *The Complete Poetry and Selected Prose of John Donne...etc.*, ed. R.S. Hillyer, New York, 1941, p. xxii.

20. *Donne's Poetical Works*, vol. ii, pp. 104-105.

21. *Satire I*, 11. 42-48.

22. See Bernard Harris, p. 191.

23. *Poetry of the English Renaissance 1509-1660*, ed. Hebel and Hudson, New York, 1929, p. 331, 11. 1-8. Contrast, also, Donne's fondling motley humorist' of *Satire I* with Marston's picture of a 'Humour' in *Satire X : Humours* from *The Scourge of Villainy*, 1598, 11. 13-29.

24. Joseph Hall's satires appeared in two parts · *Virgidemiarum's* first three books of *Toothless Satires* (1597) ; augmented in the following year by the three last books of *Biting Satires*.

25. *Poetry of the English Renaissance 1509-1660*, p. 365, 11.1-16.

CHAPTER IV

Elegies

I

The relative indifference of critics to Donne's *Elegies* provides an excellent point for starting our examination of these poems. Among books exclusively on Donne, as far as I know, only J. B. Leishman's *The Monarch of Wit* goes into these poems in some detail. The characteristic critical attitude towards the *Elegies* is well illustrated by K. W. Gransden. Of them he says :

> Their characteristics are vigour, concrete imagery, a set of psychological attitudes found also in some the more cynical of the *Songs and Sonnets*, and a particular conventional morality or rather amorality proper to this form of literary exercise (all husbands should be cuckolded, all women are fickle) which expresses itself in the confident artificiality of the situations employed. Most of these features, except the racy and masterful use of language, which is purely Donne's and *which is the sole reason we read the poems*, were inherited from Ovid.[1] *(italics mine)*

This may be ascribed to prejudices that have lingered even to this day on account of certain emphases. Donne's *Elegies*, it has been assumed, were written in the same spirit as his prose *Paradoxes and Problems*; they are just academic exercises and evaporations of wit. Joan Bennett regards the

Elegies and the cynical poems among the *Songs and Sonnets*, like his prose *Paradoxes and Problems*, as products of the confusion of realism with cynicism that inevitably occurs when realism is sought as an escape from idealisation. 'One affectation is replaced by its opposite.' The characteristics of these poems are 'intellectual exuberance and a spirit of contradiction.' Both the prose and verse writings of Donne in this mood are 'exercises in moral paradox,' which 'compensate for cold affectation by bright wit and ingenious logic.'[2]

Though Joan Bennett admits that Donne was 'a shrewd observer and even his lightest writings are apt to contain... flashes of insight', she also asserts in no uncertain terms that in these writings 'Donne has his tongue in his cheek.'[3] There is no doubt some truth in what she says, for the Elizabethans developed brilliant paradoxes which, even while arguing from established axioms, made conventional morality stand on its head. The young wits of the age were ostentatious in their parade of immorality and with them the *Elegies* and similar other poems of Donne would be, like his little, unserious prose essays, immensely popular on account of their purpose of giving a feeling of participation in something delightfully wicked.[4] This is not denying the importance of what J. B. Leishman calls 'sheer wit'[5] which pervades almost all the poetry of Donne and is particularly apparent in the poems we are considering. It should be remembered that it was this element of 'sheer wit' which seems to have made the greatest impression on Donne's contemporaries, even when, like Jonson and Drummond, they were poets whose own ideals and achievements were very different. However, too exclusive an emphasis on only this narrow meaning of the term in relation to Donne's *Elegies* has, by encouraging the feeling that these poems need not be taken seriously because in them Donne is only participating in a game—playing with certain aspects (all of them undesirable) of the relationship between the sexes—and using them with a devastating scepticism to display his mental dexterity in puncturing traditional ideals, perpetuated the indifference to these poems.

On the other hand, Donne's *Elegies* have been treated too often as entries in a diary, and this has given rise to some interesting speculations about Donne's possible lecheries in his youth. Taken as such, the *Elegies* seem to tell us autobiographically of 'wild living and licentious wooing,' and once their relationship with ths poet's life has been established, it is believed, they may be safely dismissed. To Edmund Gosse some of the *Elegies* seem to form a group recording the experience of Donne's intrigue with some married women during 1596 and 1597.[6] Arthur Quiller-Couch goes further and observes :

> It may have been in prudence, being under suspicion, that in 1596, John cleared from London and joined in the Earl of Essex's famous expedition to Cadiz. Quite as likely it was to avoid the scandal of more worldly transgressions: for his poems (and Ben Jonson tells us that he wrote all his best pieces of verse before twenty-five) tell us autobiographically of wild living and licentious wooing :

> Th' expense of spirit in a waste of shame... and of shamelessness, we may add. They exhibit him as a genuine heir of the Renaissance, insatiable alike in carnal and intellectual curiosity ; mad to possess, and, having possessed, violent in reaction, crueller . . . than Horace to his castaways, then even more cruelly, cynically, cold in analysing the ashes of disgust.

The *Elegies* and the love poetry of Donne, we are told, reflect his own wild life as a young man. Donne himself has, it is argued, pleaded guilty to a careless and passionate youth :

In mine idolatry what showers of rain
Mine eyes did waste? What griefs my heart did rent ?
That sufference was my sin; now I repent ;
'Cause I did suffer I must suffer pain.
Th' hydroptique drunkard, and night-scouting thief,
The itchy Lecher, and self tickling proud
Have the remembrance of past joys, for relief
Of coming ills.

(*Holy Sonnet III*. 11.5-12)

But there is actually no satisfactory evidence to prove that Donne had a dissipated or immoral youth.[8]   However, from what we know of the lives of Essex, Raleigh, Southampton, Pembroke, and others, it is probable that Donne's *Elegies* came quite close to the truth of the life of the time.   The later cantos of *The Fairy Queen* reflect vividly the unchaste loves and troubled friendships of Elizabeth's Court.[9]   In regarding Donne's *Elegies* as autobiography there is the 'danger of making an attractive romance about him,'[10] a possibility of exaggerating the erotic element in them and thus overlooking the more important fact that they are not confessions but poems.

To many of us the interest of poetry is perhaps enhanced by its reflection of the poet's life. To conjecture that particular poems belong to particular episodes in the poet's life is a fascinating pursuit. But this has been indulged in too much. It has led to few certainties and cannot in any case do much to increase our appreciation of the poetry. On the contrary, it has encouraged an extra-literary interest in the *Elegies*. The relationship of almost all these poems with Donne's actual life is insoluble and perhaps unimportant. Some of them need only to be thought of as witty exercises and others as expressions of moments of intense emotional activity inside the poet's mind—that is, they have either no correspondence to reality, or, if they succeed as poetry, their only correspondence is to an inner reality, existing in the poet's mind, not to any biographically identifiable facts. Although the poems are love poems, it is not necessary to search for the source of their inspiration in actual people or incidents. One or two of the *Elegies*, by their tenderness and unwonted gentleness, may be associated with Anne More ; the note of intrigue and bitterness in others might suggest them to have been addressed to the married woman with whom Donne is supposed to have had an intrigue and who later earned his contempt by her faithlessness ; and one was, on Walton's testimony, written as a tribute to Mrs. Herbert. But, above all, they are works of art, explorations of the love-relationship from, of course, the man's point of view. They should be read as poems, each complete in itself, as a real object capable of being admired and studied alone on the page ; not as clues to the poet's life. A poem of any merit cannot depend on anything but itself. Only by approaching the *Elegies* in this spirit may we know their literary worth and the position they occupy among the whole body of Donne's poems.

The probable dates of Donne's *Elegies*[11] indicate their relatively early composition, like that of the satires, among his poems, and this, I believe, is the most important reason for beginning a study of Donne's love poems with his *Elegies*. Here is immediately apparent the 'sheer wit', which plays an important part in almost all of Donne's poetry, as also the genesis of his characteristic technique in which wit goes beyond mere striving after clever logical effects and moral paradox and becomes the all-embracing impulse of the creative mind, a quality of imagination itself, and though working through 'the subtle and fantastic web of dialectic' and abstractions, yet gives a strong and vivid sense of realism by portraying 'a passion which is not ideal nor conventional, neither recollected in tranquillity nor a pure product of literary fashion, but love as an actual, immediate experience,'[12] a variously mooded passion working through a swift and subtle brain. In these earliest lyrics of Donne we can see, as we have already done in his satires, his desire to speak out in his own voice; and though for the model of his lyric he turned, indeed, to the conventional Elizabethan form, he creates his own modes, modes which do not come to him readymade but arise out of the artistic pressures of the moment. The most striking thing about them is their extraordinary realism, their freedom from the conventional ornaments of poetry. They have very few metaphors or images or illustrations. In them Donne is not concerned with what Petrarch, or Ronsard, or Spenser, or the courtly Italian Platonists might have said about love : indeed, he is not even concerned with what Ovid, to whom he is supposed to have been indebted for at least the triangular situations we find in some of his *Elegies*, might have said about love. He is concerned with only his perception of the various aspects of man-woman relationship and with the expression of this, sometimes directly and at other times through the analogy of concrete reality and abstract idea, but conveying by means of the manner of speech and the nature of argument the sense of the duality of an identifiable individual who is involved at more than the mere intellectual level and is capable of willingly and constantly putting himself in another's place and regarding himself with amused detachment. The emotion is abstracted into an idea and then the idea is made to retain its feeling-tone through the poet's imagination which is primarily dramatic, with the consequence that the poems have the emotion vividly and concretely and at the same time refined by the reflective power. When wit functions thus, it produces poetry which is fantastic, witty, and original without being affected, trivial, and absurd. It makes no sense outside the realm of poetry where it is created, that is, outside the poem. It is empirically meaningless, but it produces a brilliant and curiously moving poem, for although it may combine argument, impudence, paradox, and ingenuity, it results into something which comes to more than their sum total without suppressing any one of them.

It cannot be pretended, of course, that all of Donne's *Elegies* are illustrations of wit in this wider and deeper sense. About half of the *Elegies* are essentially in the same spirit as we find in the *encomias* and paradoxes cited by J. B. Leishman in *The Monarch of Wit*[13] and which were so popular at the time of Donne.[14] These are poems primarily witty rather than dramatic. In seven of them, namely, *The Anagram, Change, The Comparison, The Bracelet, Variety,* and "Oh, let me not serve so", the wit is 'logical, argumentative, scholastic,' employed either to defend some indefensible propositions or just for the sake of dialectical exercise. *The Autumnal,* a complimentary poem which some believe to have been addressed to Mrs. Herbert, also belongs to this group. In the rest, that is, *Love's Progress, Going to Bed,* and *Love's War,* the Wit is Ovidian. Perhaps it is too much of a simplification to categorise the *Elegies* or any other poems of Donne into such neat divisions. The more one reads his poems, especially the love poems, the more one sees the folly of classifications. Even in *The Anagram,* that preposterous defense of a preposterous idea, which we have classified as dialectically witty rather than dramatic, there is something dramatic, for here 'Donne is not merely maintaining a paradox, but also, as it were, playing the part of the sort of man who would maintain such a paradox.'[15] The same may be said of that Ovidian lyric, *Love's Progress.* On the other hand, the distinctly dramatic *Elegies* have elements that are found in the predominantly witty ones, argument paradox, and impudence or outrageousness. However' broadly speaking, the *Elegies* which we have described as witty conform to a conventional Elizabethan practice of the form known as elegy. In Elizabethan England, as in Augustan Rome, the amatory elegy did not always wail or moan,[16] for like their predecessors, love-smitten Englishmen 'gave the name of elegy to their pleasantries as well as lamentations.'[17] William Webb's *Discourse of English Poetry* (1586) assured its readers that 'light matters, as Epigrams and Elegies' were written 'with much pleasant dalliance,' and that the elegiac verse 'serveth especially to the handling of love and dalliances, whereof it taketh the name.'[18] He made the matter even more explicit. Grouping all poetry into three categories—'Comical, Tragical and Historical,' he continued, 'Under the first all such Epigrams, Elegies, and delectable ditties which poets have devised respecting only the delights thereof : in the second, all doleful complaints, lamentable chances, and whatsoever else is poetically expressed in sorrow and heaviness.'[19] Songs of dalliance and the delights thereof are the three *Elegies* of Fletcher's *Licia*, which represent a love that is anything but thwarted. This also is the distinctive note of Donne's *Elegies*, which we have denominated as witty, and of some of the *Songs and Sonnets*, such as "Go, and catch a falling star", *Woman's Constancy*, and *The Indifferent*—as also of some others in a similar unserious vein in which the poet enlarges wittly on woman's faithlessness or exhibits his own inconstancy.

But not all of Donne's *Elegies* belong to the category of love's dalliance and delights thereof. 'To this melancholy Dean,' J.W. Draper remarks, 'variety was the very spice of art; and the urge for the unusual displayed itself not only in the preciousness of his style but in the paradox of his themes; and to produce this piquancy of the unexpected, his poetry becomes a sort of chameleon's dish, an *olla* of attitudes towards his two favourite subjects.'[20] Donne's poems are very difficult to classify, for he seems to love hybrids and violates the bounds of poetic definitions. Presently the note of dalliance gives way to a variety of experiences represented dramatically. *The Perfume* is a poem of intrigue. *The Expostulation*, starting with an accusation, goes on to cursing and finally to love-making. *The Dream* expresses thwarted love. *Jealousy* and "Nature's lay Idiot" are expressions of bitterness and scorn for an unfaithful mistress. *His parting from her.* *On his Mistress,* and *His Picture* have a feeling of tenderness and sincerity. The development perceptible through the *Elegies* also indicates a slowly increasing mastery of craft.

II

The Anagram, one of the seven elegies which we have described earlier as mainly witty rather than dramatic, has been compared by Drummond with Tasso's *Stanzas against Beauty*.[21] Both the poems belong to the tradition of academic wit. Leishman has dwelt elaborately upon the origin of the paradoxical style of Donne in *The Anagram*.[22] In this poem, as also in *The Comparison,* the poet has neatly mocked, in his description of Flavia, the convention of dividing the whole into parts, which we all use constantly, producing imagery in the process. The tone is still conversational because of the argumentative intention of the poem, but it does not project a character except in a very general way.

Donne almost certainly had Tasso's stanzas[23] in mind while he composed *The Anagram.* But more important than similarities are the differences between the two poems. The only really astonishing thing about Tasso's poem is the initial paradox that ugliness in a woman is better than beauty, but the following defense of this paradox is confined mainly to statements or arguments developed in a languid manner, in which we can perceive at least some truth. There is a certain reasonableness and moderation in Tasso's paradox. Donne, on the other hand, flings moderation to the winds and overwhelms us with an array of short analogical or syllogistic arguments which follow one another so rapidly that we have scarcely time to detect or to protest against fallacies. Some of the analogies are compressed syllogisms :

> All love is wonder; if we justly do
> Account her wonderful, why not lovely too ?
>
> (11. 25-26)

The proposition that 'All that is lovable is wonderful' does not include the corrollary, which is necessary to the conclusion: 'All that is wonderful is lovable.' Donne begins with established axioms and then tricks us into a fallacious conclusion. This is the kind of wit that is found in his *Paradoxes and problems*. The poem has an affinity with the convention of learned fooling of the later Renaissance. Donne, who probably returned at the age of nineteen or so from an Italy where the game had been made very popular by Berni and others, seems to have been the first important English poet to fully exploit its possibilities, and his originality in this respect consists largely in the fact that he introduced into the already popular game something of the rigidly logical and systematic method of the academic or theological disputation. One might say, in fact, that he played the game according to far stricter and more difficult rules than it had ever been played with before.[24]

The Comparison (*Elegy VIII*) is again a parody of the convention of dividing the whole into parts, producing images in the process which are here, strictly speaking, a series of ingenious and often rather nauseous comparisons between the poet's pretended mistress and someone else's. My mistress's sweat, the poet declares, is like (among many other nice things) attar of roses; your mistress's is like (among many other nasty things) the scum which Sancerra's starving citizens extracted from parboiled boots. My mistress's head is as round as the apple which Paris awarded to Venus, or like the apple which Eve tasted; your mistress's head is like that of a rough-hewn jet statue. And so on, for more than fifty lines. The vivid and concentrated detail in several of these comparisons, together with the element of exaggeration and caricature, is quite in the manner of some of the descriptions in Ben Jonson's comedies. But while Jonson's comparisons, as ingenious and striking as Donne's, are uttered in the right situation, the resemblances displayed in The *Comparison* exist merely for themselves and for the sake of ingenuity :

Thine's like worm eaten trunks, cloth'd in seal's skin,
Or grave, that's dust without, and stink within.
And like that slender stalk, at whose end stands
The woodbine quivering, are her arms and hands.
Like rough bark'd elm boughs, or the russet skin
Of men late scourg'd for madness, or for sin,
Like Sun-parch'd quarters on the city gate,
Such is thy tann'd skin's lamentable state.

(11. 25-32)

In the same way, *Elegy VI* ("Oh, let me not serve so") seems to exist chiefly for the sake of clever comparisons. The 'faithless thee' is like a whirlpool, a taper, and the devil :

So, careless flowers strew'd on the water's face,
The curled whirlpools suck, smack, and embrace,
Yet drown them; so, the taper's beamy eye
Amorously twinkling, beckons the giddy fly,
Yet burns his wings; and such the devil is,
Scarce visiting them, who are entirely his.

(11. 15-20)

The comparison that follows is even more startling and lucid in its sustained involutions :

When I behold a stream, which, from the spring,
Doth with doubtful melodious murmuring,

Or in a speechless slumber. calmly ride
Her wedded channel's bosom, and then chide
And bend her brows, and swell if any bough
Do but stoop down, or kiss her upmost brow;
Yet, if her often gnawing kisses win
The teacherous bank to gape, and let her in,
She rusheth violently, and doth divorce
Her from her native, and her long-kept course,
And roars, and braves it, and in gallant scorn,
In flattering eddies promising return,
She flouts the channel, who thenceforth is dry;
Then say I; that is she, and this am I.

(11. 21-34)

The Bracelet (*Elegy XI*) was a favourite poem of Jonson[25]. According to Grierson, 'Donne has in this Elegy carried to its farthest extreme, as only a metaphysical or scholastic poet like himself could, the favourite Elizabethan pun on the coin called the Angel. Shakespeare is fond of the same quibble : "She has all the rule of her husband's purse; She hath a legion of angels." (*The Merry Wives of Windsor*, I,iii, 1.60). But Donne knows more of the philosophy of angels than Shakespeare and can pursue the analogy into more surprising subtleties. Nor is the pun on angels the only one which he follows up in this poem : crowns, pistolets, and gold are all played upon in turn.'[26]

The Bracelet is perhaps Donne's 'most astonishingly successful exercise in sheer wit.'[27] Punning throughout, as the Elizabethans were so fond of doing, upon the double meaning of 'angel', the spirit and the coin, he declares that his chief regret is that twelve righteous angels, which Heaven commanded to be his providers and guides, must be damned for offenses not their own, cast into the fire, and melted down to restore the lost chain. The following passage, turning as it does upon the kind of wisdom and knowledge possessed by fallen angels and upon the dependence of substance or being on form, may perhaps more appropriately be called scholastic or dialectical. Just as in *The Anagram* Donne has employed the argumentative method, here he uses some of the School doctrines :

> But o thou wretched finder whom I hate
> So, that I almost pity thy state:
> Gold being the heaviest metal amongst all,
> May my most heavy curse upon thee fall:
> Here fetter'd, manacled, and hang'd in chains,
> First mayst thou be; then chained to hellish pains;
> Or be with foreign gold brib'd to betray
> Thy Country, and fail both of that and thy pay.
> May the next thing thou stoop'st to reach, contain
> Poison whose nimble fume rot thy moist brain;
> Or libels, or some interdicted thing,
> Which negligently kept thy ruin bring.
> Lust-bred diseases rot thee; and dwell with thee
> Itching desire, and no ability.
> May all the evils that gold ever wrought;
> All mischiefs that all devils ever thought;
> Want after plenty; poor and gouty age;
> The plagues of travellers; love; marriage
> Afflict these, and at thy life's last moment.
> May thy swollen sins themselves to thee present.
> But, I forgive; repent thee honest man:
> Gold is Restorative, restore it then;
> But if from it thou beest loath to depart,
> Because 'tis cordial, would 'twere at thy heart.

> (11. 91-114)

A reference was made in the first chapter to the frequent recurrence of the term 'sensibility' in T.S. Eliot's "The Metaphysical Poets", and this was interpreted as indicating

Eliot's greater regard for feeling rather than thought in poetry. But Donne's poetry is too intellectual to be described by sensibility alone. However, Eliot has also gone into the problem of sensibility in several of his other writings which throw better light on his attitude towards thought. In "Andrew Marvell", for example, the wit of the metaphysical poets is defined as involving 'probably a recognition, implicit in the expression of every experience, of other kinds of experience which are possible.'[28] This is a description of a necessarily intellectual approach to experience. In his comparison of Dryden's view of the poet's imagination in the Preface to *Annus Mirabilis* with Coleridge's famous passage on the distinction between fancy and imagination in *Biographia Literaria*,[29] Coleridge's distinction is found to be an oversimplification: 'I am not sure that Coleridge has made as satisfactory an analysis as that of Dryden.'[30] Further, T.S. Eliot has said of the metaphysical poets :

Not only Cowley, but all the metaphysical poets, had very fanciful minds, and if you removed the fancy and left only imagination, as Coleridge appears to use these terms, you would have no metaphysical poetry.[31]

What Eliot means by describing the metaphysical poets as fanciful may be seen from what he has said of the function of fancy: 'Fancy is an activity of the imagination rather than of the intellect, but is necessarily in part an intellectual activity, in as much as it is a "moulding of the thought as judgement represents it proper".'[32] Thus, though Eliot does not go to the extreme extent of Herbert Read,[33] who regards metaphysical poetry as absolutely intellectual, it is an error to find in him a greater attachment to sensibility than to thought—at least when he is dealing with the metaphysical poets.[34]

Our intellectual life is a constant struggle to establish a balance and the amount of coherence we succeed in establishing between the felt and the thought determines the degree of reality apprehended by us. The mode by which Donne tries to establish this balance is dramatic, and, as we have already seen, he does not always succeed in it. When the desired balance is lost and sheer intellectual jugglery takes control, the result is a poem like *The Autumnal*, where Donne's sensibility, though manifesting tenderness, 'seems only very occasionally to modify his thought, which...might as well have been directed upon a broomstick.'[35] The thoughts in *The Autumnal* have not been imparted 'thisness' which refers to the felt side of the given—the immediate presence in feeling. This makes the whole poem unreal. But *The Autumnal* is not the example by which Donne's poetry should be judged. He is at his best when he combines experience with thought in balance and this he does in many of his love poems.

III

The group of *Elegies* possessing Ovidian wit will lead us to the central position taken up in this work. Ovid's *Amores* was undoubtedly a very important influence on Donne's love poetry. The similarities between the poets are quite perceptible. But more significant than the similarities are the dissimilarities we find in Donne, which are not quite surface but substantial, in both spirit and tone, giving to his poetry a character which is meaningfully dramatic.

Grierson has indicated the classical spirit of Donne's love poetry—'so penetrated with the sensual, realistic, scornful tone of the Latin lyric and elegiac poets.'[36] Donne's indebtedness to Ovid deserves consideration. While their techniques are different, the love which is the main burden of their songs is something very different from the ideal passion of Dante or Petrarch, or of Sidney or Spenser. It is a more sensual thing. The same tone of witty carnality runs through the works of the two poets.[37]

Thomas Carew, in his elegy on Donne, declared that the lesser poets whom Donne had left behind—

> Will repeal the goodly exil'd train
> Of gods and goddesses, which in thy just reign
> Were banish'd nobler Poems, now, with these
> The silenc'd tales o' th' Metamorphorses
> Shall stuff their lines, and swell the windy Page.[38]

At the time Donne started writing, English poetry could be regarded as suffering from several disorders. The conventions of the late Elizabethan lyric were already beginning to stifle the earlier music. The lyric writers were beautifully and subtly modulating the language in order to provide songs suitable for the composers to set. This meant that they could not risk too startling an originality. The sung verse, as we have seen in the first chapter, is to be distinguished from the spoken verse and can never carry the same amount of intellectual weight as the other can. It is essential for the listener of a song to be able to identify easily and surely the single emotional key. Thus a conventional, highly decorative and graceful vocabulary and diction became characteristic of what has been called 'The Golden Age of English Lyricism.' The language of lyric poetry became simply a series of stock emotional gestures. This was true also, to some extent, of the poems written in the Petrarchan tradition. The conventional machinery of the reluctant mistress and the complaining lover, and the equally conventional vocabulary of sighs, vows, and tears—all set in an ideal setting, caused the language of passion frequently to come very close to the language of sentimental affectation. More significantly, there was little attempt to present the real complexities of human involvement in an emotional relationship. The poems existed at a distance from actuality.[39]

While this is a very one-sided picture of the situation, this

background against which Donne reacted is important to
know for an understanding of the specific relationship between him and Ovid. If we place Donne's *Elegies* and Ovid's
Amores (Ovid's *Elegies* the Elizabethans called them) side by
side, the influence of the older poet is evident. Donne's predecessors had exploited the classical mythology and legend, and
had drawn largely on the Ovid of the *Metamorphoses*.
Donne, who despised mere ornaments and childish fancies,
proceeded to do something much more daring and original—
something, too, which was almost a complete antithesis to
that Petrarchan adoration and Platonic idealism of which,
together with classical mythology and classical allusions, he
and many of his contemporaries had had more than enough: he
proceeded to reproduce something of the tone, the situations,
and the cynical wit of Ovid's *Amores*. Although there are
important differences in style between Donne and Ovid, what
Donne succeeded in catching were 'the impudence and in-
solence and the assumptions about the true nature and end of
love and the proper attitude to husbands.' Many of his *Elegies*
and some of the *Songs ond Sonnets* appear to have derived
their situations from Ovid's *Amores*; while in some others,
though the situations are not taken from Ovid, we can still
feel his presence in the background.[40]

Love's War has affinities with at least three of Ovid's
Amores : with the ninth of the First Book in which Ovid
wittily and antithetically insists on the similarities between
the qualities of a good lover and a good soldier—such as the
capacity to endure night watches, to sleep on the ground, not
to fear the face of an enemy, to beseize and take by storm, to
surprise the enemy even in sleep, to elude watchmen and
sentries; [although it is true that Donne, unlike Ovid, is concerned not with similarities but with differences. Then there
are those impudent elegies, the tenth and the twelfth of the
Second Book in which Ovid has celebrated his bloodless
victory over Corinna, declaring that by his own generalship

98

alone he has overcome countless enemies without shedding a drop of blood and without causing a new war.

Donne has not imitated any of the verbal detail of Ovid's elegies, but some of his epigrammatic lines in *Love's War* are quite in Ovid's manner :

Other men war that they their rest may gain;
But we will rest that we may fight again.
Those wars the ignorant, these th' experienc'd love,
There we are always under, here above.
There Engines far off breed a just true fear,
Near thrusts, pikes, stabs, yet bullets hurt not here.
Their lies are wrongs; here safe uprightly lie;
There men kill men, we will make one by and by.

(11. 33-40)

Leishman remarks :

One is not aware, as one is in the dramatic elegies, as one is even in *His Picture*, which is almost a limiting case— one is not even momentarily aware of a person whom Donne is addressing and whose real or imaginary personality is to some extent dictating and qualifying what he says : one is aware only of Donne himself, wittily developing a paradox. He might just as well have addres- sed the elegy to a friend, have substituted the third person for the second, and have begun...[41]

In such criticism too much attention is paid to the witty element in the poem—to the epigrammatic brilliance of the last lines and their paradox. Really, these epigrams are given a dramatic form by the person of the speaker. The Ovidian paradox in the second part of the poem is not quite insignificant when we find it coming from a speaker whose state of mind is far from being trivial. Starting on a light note:

Till I have peace with thee, war other men,
And when I have peace, can I leave thee then ?

(11. 1-2)

The poem gradually brings us face to face with a man, shaken
and tortured by the prospect of a long and dangerous voyage
to a 'hot parching clime' which may turn him before his time
to 'dust and ashes' :

And I should be in the hot parching clime,
To dust and ashes turn'd before my time.
To mew me in a Ship, is to enthral
Me in a prison, that were like to fall;
Or in a Cloister; save that there men dwell
In a calm heaven, here in a swaggering hell.
Long voyages are long consumptions,
And ships are carts for executions.
Yea they are Deaths; Is 't not all one to fly
Into the other world, as 'tis to die ?

(11. 19-28)

Accordingly, the conceit changes from soldiery treated
in a light vein to voyaging in a serious tenor. The earlier
witty elaboration of similarities between soldiers and lovers
becomes expressive of an individual's emotion. Thus, while
it is true that in *Love's War* we are not aware of the person
addressed, it is not quite appropriate to say that there is just
Donne in the poem wittily developing a paradox. The speaker
has a character of his own which is marked clearly in the
manner of his speech and the nature of his argument.

Love's Progress again has Ovidian touch, though the ingenious comparisons Donne uses in order to describe the lover's
progress in terms of a voyage could never possibly have
occurred to Ovid or to any other classical poet. In some other
Elegies of Donne speakers show us the male animal even

more clearly, in all his absurdity and passion. *Love's Progress* is one of those elegies in which the speaker apparently simply adopts the exaggerated terminology and ideal imagery of convention in order to arouse our interest in the beauty of his mistress and our envy at his own good fortune in possessing her. Here Donne presents what appears at first sight to be merely an argument in favour of the act of love—ornamented with erotic imagery of a conventionally exaggerated kind. Upon examination, however, the poem falls into three distinct parts.

The first thirtyseven lines are devoted to an argument, couched in deliberately witty and clever terms, to prove that one should always have 'the right true end of love' in mind. Statements that one loves a woman for her virtue, beauty, or wealth are admissions of sin. Beginning impressively with—

Who ever loves, if he do not propose
The right true end of love, he's one that goes
To sea for nothing but to make him sick...

(11. 1-3)

The argument continues thus : Perfection is in unity—prefer one woman first, and then one thing in her. When the poet values gold, he may think of its ductility, application, wholesomeness, and immunity from rust and fire, but he loves it because it is the soul of trade. We may think of all these in women (if women had them) and yet love but one part of them. A woman is not virtue, beauty, or wealth, and to love a woman for these and to say so is an admission of sin. This conclusion is further supported by some high-sounding but wholly specious analogies :

Search every sphere
And firmament, our *Cupid* is not there :
He's an infernal god and under ground,

With *Pluto* dwells, where gold and fire abound :
Men to such Gods, their sacrificing Coals
Did not in Altars lay, but pits and holes.
Although we see Celestial bodies move
Above the earth, the earth we Til! and love :

(11. 28-34)

So finally it is proved :

So we her airs contemplate, words and heart,
And virtues ; but we love the Centrique part.

(11. 35-36)

The argument in the first section is unserious and yet has
a truth in it. The speaker is shown to be devoted to sexual
pleasure, but also to be impatient of high sounding nonsense
about that pleasure. He admits what he is after. It is therefore
amusing when, in lines 37-70, he indulges in a high-flown
description of a woman's beauties, beginning at the head and
journeying over the nose ('like to the first Meridian') between
two suns, across swelling lips (the 'Islands fortunate'), between 'the straight *Hellespont*' of the *Sestos* and Abydos of
her breasts, and so sailing towards 'her *India*', and finally
arriving at that 'Centrique part' of which he is so much enamoured. The language here, with its profusion of 'Paradise',
'rosy Hemisphere', *'Canaries'*, 'Ambrosial', 'Sirens', 'Delphic
Oracles', 'pearls', 'glorious Promontory', *'India'*, and 'fair
Atlantic Navel', would give us the impression that the speaker
in the poem was simply revelling in his erotic imaginings were
it not that the images are absurdly fantastic—parody, in fact.
The conventional Elizabethan love lyrics using such imagery
carefully avoid any indication of gross actuality. But the
speaker of *Love's Progress* goet out of his way to emphasise.
the actuality beneath the metaphors, and thus to throw doubt
on the sincerity of the whole rapturous catalogue. Suspicion

is turned into certainty when conventional eroticism changes into derisive bawdiness in lines 69 and 70. The voyager comes to grief and can proceed no further.

The last movement of the poem, in a style which brutally contrasts with the high seriousness of the previous section, is again argumentative. We are advised that it is better to begin our voyage at the foot rather than the head and the whole poem is challenged and coarsened by the candid vulgarity of the closing lines.

This poem is not simply a dirty story; it is an exposure of the stupidity of a too elaborate and sophisticated sexual procedure. Thus, in a poem which clearly derives from Ovid, Donne has exposed the fundamental unhealthiness of euphemistic sensuous description which are unrelated to reality and in doing so has also portrayed for use a witty lecherous young man who is impatient of the delights of mere anticipation, and who recognises bluntly and directly the simple physical necessity which lurks within all the romantic verbiage.

This is, in a sense, Donne's 'anti-poetry'—his revolt against so much which his predecessors and contemporaries regarded as poetic. It is also, however, his statement of the ambiguity in sexual love. The speaker may be derisive of romantic expressions, but he also enjoys them. He may pretend to be rational, a man with commonsense, but he is also very much attracted by hyperbolic statements. His 'rational' arguments are as exaggerated, and (in a way) as idealised, as his derisive sensual catalogue of the woman's charms. So we have, yet again, a poem that has its chief 'message' in the complexities of psychological attitudes which define the nature of a certain personality.[42]

Going to Bed (*Elegy XIX*) also in an elegy that might have been suggested by Ovid—to be specific, by the fifth in the First Book of *Amores* where he describes how Corinna came to him one hot noon while he was resting on his couch.[43] Here, though the addressee remains silent as in *Love's*

War and *Love's Progress*, and though the poet shares with the Renaissance poets 'the common refusal to narrow the task of images to that of a truthful report of experience',[44] we find again the complexities of the human mind and these are portrayed without violating the Renaissance belief in ideas as the true reality of a thinking man.

Rosemond Tuve remarks : 'The intention of Elizabethan and early seventeenth-century imagery is not chiefly to individualise, but to select such particulars as will best indicate the intended universal.'[45] This commonly held conception is familiar to us in Sidney's discussion of embellished nature : nature's world is 'brazen', the poet only delivers a 'golden.' The poet does not copy nature, but—

...lifted up with the vigour of his own invention, doth grow in effect another nature, in making things either better than Nature bringeth forth, or, quite anew, forms such as never were in Nature.... neither let this be jestingly conceived, because the works of the one be essential, the other, in limitation or fiction; for any understanding knoweth the skill of the Artificer standeth in that *Idea* or force-conceit of the work, and not in the work itself.

(*Elizabethan Critical Essays*, vol. i, pp. 155-157)

This conception of poetry would require a poet to represent not the actually experienced, but the very 'pattern and concentrated essence' of feelings like love or anger or hunger for variety. Donne replied to Jonson's complaint against his *Anniversary* with the remark that he had 'described the idea of a Woman.'[46] Indeed his poem seeks to build up a sense of intellectual and intelligible order out of a number of disparate elements. The Renaissance conception of imitating the idea, and not the actual experience, does not force him to omit apparently discordant experiences; it only forces him to

make up his mind, and subtly indicate why he has chosen to
admit them. In this way the coherence is imposed by the
poet's meaning.[47] The basis of such a poem is intellectual
and ideal—ideal in the sense of that word's affinity with *Idea*:
the ideal as opposed to the real. This constitutes the Renaissance poetic theory which Rosemond Tuve applies to *Going
to Bed* in her suggestion that the effect of the poem is not of
the particular but of the personified universal.[48] Sidney has
distinguished the poet from the philosopher :

> ...whatsoever the philosopher sayeth should be done, he
> [the poet] giveth a perfect picture of it in some one by
> whom he presupposeth it was done. So as he coupleth
> the general notion with the particular example. A perfect
> picture I say, for he yieldeth to the powers of the mind
> and image of that whereof the philosopher bestoweth but
> a wordy description ; which doth neither strike, pierce, nor
> possess the sight of the soul so much as that other doth.
>
> (*Elizabethan Critical Essays*, vol. i, p. 164)

It is true that the idea of 'Full nakedness' is apostrophised
for full fourteen lines in *Going to Bed*, with three analogies
to demonstrate why 'bodies uncloth'd must be, / To taste
whole joys.' But these lines are, in fact, only a part of the
pattern offered by the poem and in no way obstruct psychological realism. Donne uses the real which is particular and it
is the ideal only in the sense of the idea, as that to which all
concrete offspring or exemplars must, to make sense, be ultimately and implicitly related. In a way Donne's aim is, it may
be said, to realise the ideal. But as even Plato has admitted,
the ideal can only be approached through the 'real' which is
its shadow—the world of touch, taste, sight, and sense. We
have already referred to Sidney's distinction between the poet
and the philosopher on the ground that the poet combines
the 'general notion' with the 'particular example.'[49]

Apparently, *Going to Bed* is a straightforward erotic elegy.
The exaggerated language of the poem is at first productive
of an atmosphere of half-amused tenderness :

Your gown going off, such beauteous state reveals,
As when from flow'ry meads th' hill's shadow steals.
Off with that weary Coronet and show
The hairy Diadem which on you doth grow:
Now off with those shoes, and then safely tread
In this love's hallow'd temple, this soft bed.
In such white robes, heaven's Angels us'd to be
Received by men ; Thou Angel bringst with thee
A heaven like Mahomet's Paradise...
(11. 13-21)

The hyperbole is there, just faintly absurd. This absurdity is
allowed to come out in the bawdry, though of an affectionate
nature, suggested in the opening lines and again at the end
of the first movement which is a recognition of the actual
facts of physical love.

The pattern is repeated in the second movement of the
poem :

Licence my roving hands, and let them go,
Before, behind, between, above, below.
O my America ! my new-found-land,
My kingdom, safeliest when with one man mann'd,
My Mine of precious stones, My Emperie,
How blest am I in this discovering thee !
To enter in these bonds, is to be free ;
Then where my hand is set, my seal shall be.
(11. 25-32)

It is against this background of the realities of physical
love that we should view the apostrophe to 'Full nakedness'

in lines 33-46, and then it would be seen that the effect is of the particular and not of a personified universal. Whatever sense of generalisation is produced by the apostrophe is wiped away by the last two lines. The poem moves within the logic of particulars and the responses of a person involved in a real situation—the whole formulated in the pattern of a scene in drama with a character reacting to an immediate circumstance.

The situation of *Jealousy* (*Elegy I*) also comes from Ovid's *Amores*. Grierson has quoted Ovid (*Amores* : I and IV; 11. 15-32 and 51-54) to indicate that Donne must have received the suggestion for lines 19-20 and 21 f. of his elegy from the Latin poet.[50] But, on the other hand, the difference between the two poets is plain to see. There is the same tone of witty depravity in both, but whereas Ovid develops his theme with ease and grace, the lines of Donne are rough and vehement. Ovid passes from one natural and simple thought to another, methodically and exhaustively working out his subject; but Donne is subtle and extravagant, writing to create an effect of gripping immediacy. Donne partly owes the sensual, realistic, and scornful tone, which we find in most of his elegies and satires and even in some of the *Songs and Sonnets*, to Ovid, but his interest is not like Ovid's, descriptive and epigrammatic ; he usually develops his theme dramatically.[51]

The dramatic mode of Donne is illustrated by the opening lines of *Jealousy* :

Fond woman, which would'st have thy husband die,
And yet complain'st of his great jealousy ;
If swollen with poison, he lay in 'his last bed,
His body with a sere-bark covered,
Drawing his breath, as thick and short, as can
The nimblest crocheting Musician,
Ready with loathsome vomiting to spew

His soul out of one hell, into a new,
Made deaf with his poor kindreds' howling cries,
Begging with few feign'd tears, great legacies,
Thou would'st not weep, but jolly, 'and frolic be,
As a slave, which tomorrow should be free;
Yet weep'st thou, when thou see'st him hungrily
Swallow his own death, heart's-bane Jealousy.

(11. 1-14)

Donne's dramatic intention governs his choice and use of imagery. Since he aims at a vivid and rapid enactment of a situation charged with intense feeling, rather than description, he does not use a cluster as may be found anywhere in Spenser. In fact, much of the power of the first fourteen lines of the poem arises from the economy of imagery changing in rapid succession and creating startling effects. These lines are virtually in the form of an Elizabethan 'aside', for it is impossible that a lover could speak out such sentiments to a mistress with whom he evidently intends to continue his affair. After the opening lines there follows the stark picture (visualised by the lover) of the dying husband, poisoned by his treacherous wife, his body covered with 'a sere-bark' (a visual image—so rare in Donne), and drawing his breath thickly and shortly.[52] It is action (the difficult breathing of a dying man) that is suggested by the comparison in lines 5-6. It compresses into it more than one attitude and acquires an explosive power. If there is in it scorn for the cruel woman who has brought her husband to this end and a sense of pity for the suffering man, there is conversely also a conscious contempt for him, subtly indicated by 'nimblest crocheting' which is an epithet for 'musician.' With the same economy and force the rest of the scene is completed, one action-image quickly and surely coming after the other. 'Ready with loathsome vomiting to spew/His Soul out of one hell, into a new,' brings to life all the horror of the situation by its brutal realism. The same is the case in the next two lines which portray the helpless suffering of the dying man and the utter callousness of the selfish relatives. The last four lines complete the picture. These are all examples of what Alice Brandenburg has termed the 'dynamic' image, of which the chief constituent is motion, a characteristic found most often in imagery employed in drama.[53]

In the second part of the poem we feel a marked difference from the first. Whereas the first section represents the growth of a certain consciousness in the speaker, the second contains an overt counsel to the mistress and the imagery in this part is consequently of a different nature and arrangement. Gone are the violent jerks from one image to another. The cadence now changes because of the cool logical approach. Images clearly expressive of contempt for the husband are used : 'swollen and pamper'd,' 'snorts', and 'cag'd in his basket chair.' The lover tells his mistress that they should not kiss and play in her husband's house, for this is 'His realm, his castle, and his diocese.' So the lovers would, like those who revile their prince and counterfeit his currency in another land, make love in another house where they can flout the husband as the people on the right side of the Thames flout the Mayor of London—or the Germans flout the Pope. What we find in this poem is, therefore, a gradual degeneration of drama into mere wit.

The mistress in *His Parting from her* (*Elegy XII*) is again a married woman, and once more the lines describing the secret signs between the lovers seem to have been written with a poem of Ovid's *Amores* (from which Grierson has quoted in his note on *Jealousy*) in mind. On the other hand the wit of *His Parting from her* is directed only against the husband who is however, taken more seriously than the one in *Jealousy* :

Was 't not enough, that thou didst hazard us

To paths in love so dark, so dangerous :
And those so ambush'd round with household spies,
And over all, thy husband's towering eyes
That flam'd with oily sweat of jealousy :....

(11. 39-43)

The wit of the poem is not to be doubted; the mock-romantic Ovidian 'hero' even speaks in couplets in on antithetical manner. But in the address to the woman and in the speaker's discourse on their love there is a real tenderness, and he speaks with a passion and purpose that increase in intensity as the poem goes on. There is here, along with wit an intensification of material, which, it is highly interesting— although irrelevant—to speculate, came 'perhaps out of his [Donne's] own experience.'[54] The more important thing is the interesting situation portrayed in the poem, which reveals itself on closer examination. The speaker is discovered to possess contradictions which make him something more than just a symbolic exposure of the conventional poetic weakness of elevating the commonplace to the plane of the heroic and of putting the gloss of plausible, high-sounding interpretations on unpleasant facts. The creation of a character, whose individuality is revealed in sudden shifts of attention, self-deceptions, changes of tone, and failures of speech, can easily be within the large framework of a drama, but to have it within the narrow confines of a lyric is indeed a remarkable achievement of Donne. The variations in the character make the poem ambiguous. The satire coexists, with the sympathy we feel for the essential simplicity with which the lover deludes himself, and with the sense of actuality that the commonplace in the poem gives to his situation. In this poem Donne has travelled far from the Ovidian elegy, which proceeds in a much more direct manner and is not concerned with expressing psychological subtleties.

The hero of the poem begins with a more or less conventional statement of his feelings, making use of literary terms like 'Cinthia', 'Venus', 'torments', 'hell', and 'fires.' This prepares us to anticipate the usual Elizabethan figure of a complaining lover. But we have a rude shock by a sudden alteration in the tone of the speaker. He admits past promiscuity and faces the situation with more than usual frankness :

> No. no. The fault was mine, impute it to me,
> Or rather to conspiring destiny,
> Which (since I lov'd for form before) decreed,
> That I should suffer when I lov'd indeed :
> And therefore now, sooner than I can say,
> I saw the golden fruit, 'tis rapt away.
> Or as I had watched one drop in a vast stream,
> And I left wealthy only in a dream.

(11. 21-28)

The admission makes us more understanding of the lover, for we realise that he is capable of self-examination and of humility. It also makes his language of complaint appear to be at once sincere and absurd. Such an impression is confirmed a few lines later. After the couplet in which love is accused of making the lovers 'shy and glow, and pant, and burn', and a further couplet alluding to the 'paths in love so dark, so dangerous', a trite intrigue appears in lines 41-56, in which the language of high passion is used for a slyly and hypocritically conducted affair. There has been correspondence 'whilst the foe stood by'; the lovers have tasted the so much sweeter pleasures of stolen endearments; they have held 'dialogues with...feet' under the table, and employed the lovers' devices of 'becks, winks, looks.' In spite of these, however, the lover does not find it incongruous to refer to the 'Constancy' of their love, or to suggest that their clandestine goings-on deserve to be called 'Art' and not be regarded as a vulgar story. He finds nothing improper in the language he

uses and, indeed, goes on to suggest in an almost extrava-
gantly physical language, which not only reflects his intense
feeling but also indicates the complete absence of self-
consciousness in him, that their lips should grow together,
their arms lock together like ivy, and their fear freeze them
together before fortune parts them. In ostentatious terms of
dignity he says :

> Rend us in sunder, those canst not divide
> Our bodies so, but that our souls are ti'd....,
>
> (11. 69-70)

and then makes a rejoinder in a more practical tone, thus
rounding off his individuality :

> And we can love by letters still and gifts,
> And thoughts and dreams; Love never wanteth shifts.
>
> (11. 71-72)

In *His Picture* (*Elegy V*), one of the two among Donne's
Elegies which do not have a tone of witty depravity (the
other is the tenth elegy, *The Dream*), a lover, going abroad to
war, bids farewell to his mistress. So one may like to think
of it as having been written before Donne's departure with the
Cadiz expedition in June, 1596. But such a hypothesis may
at best be only incidental to an appreciation of the poem. It
is immaterial whether the poet has here represented a situation
that really happened or is purely fictitious. The work has to
be judged by what it holds and on its own merit.

The situation of this dramatic piece is that of a lover
bidding farewell before going abroad to war. After giving her
his picture, his likeness at present, he shifts quickly from the
conventional thought of his possible death to a vivid description of how he may look on his return:

> When weather-beaten I come back; may hand,
> Perhaps with rude oars torn, or Sun beams tann'd,

My face and breast of haircloth, and may head
With care's rash sudden storms, being o'erspread,
My body 'a sack of bones, broken within,
And powder's blue stains scatter'd on my skin;...

(11. 5-10)

In sensuously apprehensible images, and with passionate dignity and strength, in the last two lines the lover visualises what he will be when he comes back from the wars. Images such as these do not, however, serve usefully in the kind of poetry Donne has written—a poetry the subjects and the forms of which do not admit of leisurely elaboration or damand the painter's kind of *illustratio et evidentia*.[55]

But, that the intention of Donne in *His Picture* is neither narration nor description is evident from the brevity of the lover's visualisation and his sudden transition [to the argument —the theme of the poem—that what lovers seek in each other is love. There is here, as in other dramatic poems of Donne, the complexity of a growing situation, and this kind of thing requires dialectic. As the lover gives his mistress the picture and describes how he may look on his return, he puts into her mouth what he hopes she would say to those who wondered at her for loving a man, so 'foul, and coarse' :

This shall say what I was : and thou shalt say,
Do his hurts reach me ? doth my worth decay ?
Or do they reach his judging mind, that he
Should now love less, what he did love to see ?
That which in him was fair and delicate,
Was but the milk, which in love's childish state
Did nurse it : who now is grown strong enough
To feed on that, which to disused tastes seem tough.

(11. 13-20)

The sequence of thought is quite direct, leading to the affirmation by the mistress that when young and childish, her love had fed on the outward beauty of her lover's form and face, but that now, when it is mature and strong, it can live on the 'meat' of his inner self, which is too hard for beginners in love to relish.[56] From this, while we do not find much about her worldly circumstances, whether she is married or not, nor is there any indication that she represents some actual woman in Donne's life, we do know something more important. We know the kind of woman she is, from the earnest address of her lover as well as from the speech he puts into her mouth. She is a woman who seeks a 'judging mind' in her lover rather than physical beauty.

A similar theme is developed with far greater subtlety and beauty, and with a different set of images, in *Air and Angels*; that what the lover seeks ultimately in the beloved is love. However, mystical doctrines do not make these poems mystical. It is only that poems like these rest on the mystical assumption that love is the supreme mode of knowing, and that it produces an intense experience of release from the self and a sense of fulfilment in union with another.

The Dream (*Elegy X*), surely one of the most pleasing and memorable of Donne's elegies, is a revealing example of what was said before of his poetic mode, that he does not merely include the 'idea' in his poetic imagination but his imagination is also dramatic. It is by the dramatic nature of the poem and the accompanying rhetoric that he achieves the identity of abstract idea and concrete reality, of feeling and reflection.

It seems reasonable to suppose that the 'Image of her whom I love', addressed in the first eight lines, is not an actual picture, not a material and objectively visible portrait, but a mental picture and, in the second place, an abstract, metaphysical 'idea' such as Donne had in mind when he wrote *The Anniversaries*.[57] There are several difficulties in interpreting the elegy addressed to a picture. It is rather odd on the part of the speaker to say that he loves the picture better than the woman herself, especially since the statement is left unex-

plained. There are some other difficulties, too, in regarding the
'Image' as material and objectively visible. Why does *'Reason'*
depart when the picture is gone, since the picture can in no
way inhibit the lover's phantasies in sleep. Again, at the end
of the poem, why should it be said that the picture is like
'life's *Taper'* passing 'too fast away' ? Not only are these
difficulties removed but the meaning of the poem is accentuated if we regard the 'Image' as the Platonic 'fairer form'
which is found represented in Spenser's *Hymn in Honour of
Love*. This interpretation seems correct, for the first five
lines of the poem remind one forcibly of Platonic 'Forms' or
'Ideas', with reference to which alone objects of sense have
any meaning. Elizabeth Drury is turned into such an idea in
The Second Anniversary :

> ...she whose rich beauty lent
> Mintage to other beauties for they went
> But for so much as they were like to her;...

(11. 23-25)

This dual significance of 'Image' is the basis of the thought
expressed in *The dream'* after line 5. The identity of the
concrete and the abstract is basic to the construction of the
poem.

It is a characteristic of Donne, as we find also in *The
Extasy, Air and Angels,* and *The Undertaking,* to separate the
body from the soul and consider each as sensuously perceived. *The Dream* represents the separation of two degrees
of reality—applied to the Platonic ideal of love. The identity
of symbols is obvious. The 'Image' is the Platonic Form, or
in the words of Donne—'fair impression.' The 'she' of the
first line stands for the lady's physical entity and her beautiful
exterior. 'Whose' in line 2 may be referring to either the
'Image' (this is indicated by punctuation) which has got
impressed on the lover's 'faithful heart' and made him of the

same 'value', or to 'she' (this way less violence is done to normal grammatical structure) —in which case the meaning is that as the first step of Platonic adoration her beautiful exterior had already conquered the lover's heart before he loved her 'fairer form' or 'Image.' Her love has made the lover as 'Kings do coins, to which their stamps impart/The value.'

The man then finds that the Platonic ideal is too elevated for the earthly desires which still possess him, and begs the image (identified with 'my heart' which bears her 'fair impression' : an identification of the abstract and the concrete in a synecdoche) to leave :

...go, and take my heart from hence,
Which now is grown too great and good for me :
Honours oppress weak spirits, and our sense
Strong objects dull; the more, the less we see.

(11. 5-8)

When it is gone, and 'Reason' along with it, 'Fantasy' predominates and the lover can enjoy his mistress unhampered by their Platonic relationship. The pleasures of possessing her in dream are then described and the lover prefers these to the painful truth that she would refuse him in real life :

So, if I dream I have you, I have you,
For, all our joys are but fantastical.
And so I 'scape the pain, for pain is true;
And sleep which locks up sense, doth lock out all.
After a such fruition I shall wake,
And, but the waking, nothing shall repent;
And shall to love more thankful Sonnets make,
Than if more *honour*, *tears*, and *pains* were spent.

(11. 13-20)

Finally, with a typical Donnian turn the lover reverses himself and begs the 'Image' to stay :

But dearest heart, and dearer image stay;
Alas, true joys at best are *dreams* enough;
Though you stay here you pass too fast away :
For even at first life's *Taper* is a snuff.
Fill'd with a love, may I be rather grown
Mad with much *heart*, than *idiot* with none.

(11. 21-26)

It is easy to see the connection between this poem and the Platonic verses supposed to be addressed to friends and patronesses such as Magdalen Herbert and the Countess of Bedford. Its tone and theme are similar to those of *The Blossom*. There is something playful in both and there is a proposed separation represented with somewhat the same imagery. Again, the same amorous compliments are found here as in *Twickenham Garden*; and the same complimentary hopeless love exhibited as in *The Primrose*. Like *The Blossom*, *Confined Love*, and *The Flea*, *The Dream* springs from the thwarting of the lover's physical desire. But whereas in the other poems the disappointment of the lover leads to satire, *The Dream* escapes satire by attempting to conceive a union on a more abstract plane. Consequently the vivid drama of sensual passion is retained and at the same time refined by the reflective power. Moreover, the abstractness of the poem does not in any way deprive it of concreteness and full emotional significance, for, the imagination which is the basis of the poem is not only concrete but also dramatic.[58] The rhetoric, the outward verse form of the poem, is guided by the necessities of dramatic exposition. The first eight lines give the situation and the remaining part of the poem is devoted to an examination of the implications of the situation. There is no apparent progression in the poem, and whatever little there may be is due to the ratiocination arising out of the given situation, and this leads to a disintegrating structure. Drama in fact, is the most significant constituent of the poem, for

without this the intricate metaphysical patterns we get here
cannot be concretised and become aesthetically satisfying.

The Expostulation (Elegy XV) raises a question, which is
whether the poem was composed by Jonson or Donne. One
of the most difficult problems in Jonson's *Underwoods* is
presented by the group of elegies which occupy pages 202-
207 of the 1640 Folio (numbered lvii-lx by Gifford; xxxviii-xli
by Herford). Gifford ascribes them all to Jonson, but he
quotes Whalley's note pointing out that the second poem of
the group had been published among Donne's poem. B. H.
Newdigate also accepts Gifford's position. He states that
'Jonson's muse is sometimes so like Donne's that on merely
literary grounds it would be rash to ascribe any of these four
Elegies to one rather than to the other. Their presence in
"Under-Wood" is a strong reason for accepting them as
Jonson's.'[59]

The editors of Donne are, however, unanimous in claiming
Herford's xxxix (printed as *Elegy XV, The Expostulation*, by
Grierson) as a genuine work of that poet. Grierson is so
certain of this that he does not deem it necessary to argue in
its support; he has unreservedly included it in the canon of
Donne's undoubted poems in his authoritative edition.[60]

If we compare *The Expostulation* and Jonson's *Elegy
XXXVIII* we can see that the first could not have been written
by Jonson. In *Elegy XXXVIII*, " 'Tis true, I'm broke!'', the
addressed lady—whoever she was—appears to have had a
love affair with the poet who, in a moment of intoxication,
has betrayed her confidence and disclosed the secret of their
liaison, and is now begging for her mercy by reminding her
that she is a divinity and that divinities are merciful:

I will not stand to justify my fault,
Or lay the excuse upon the Vintner's vault;
Or in confessing of the Crime be nice,
Or go about to countenance the vice,

By naming in what company 'twas in,
As I would urge Authority for sin.
No, I will stand arraign'd, and cast, to be
The Subject of your Grace in pardoning me,
And (Still'd your mercy's Creature) will live more
Your honour now, than your disgrace before.
Think it was frailty, Mistress, think me man,
Think that your self like heaven forgive me can,
Where weakness doth offend, and virtue grieve,
There greatness takes a glory to relieve.
Think that I once was yours, or may be now,
Nothing is vile, that is a part of you:
Error and folly in me may have crost
Your just commands; yet those, not I be lost.

(Underwoods —1640 Folio —pp. 202-203)

There is no poem of Donne in which he thus humiliates himself before his mistress or begs for her forgiveness. It was partly his reaction against the Petrarchan convention (in which the woman is 'mistress' and the lover her 'servant', and which we find employed in *Elegy XXXVIII*) and partly a question of temperament. Throughout his elegies Donne addresses the woman in disdain or on equal terms, but never regards her as superior— as Jonson does. He uses forms of address such as 'Fond woman' (*Elegy I*), 'Nature's lay Idiot', and 'Fool' (*Elegy VII*), and when he is in a tenderer mood, the woman becomes 'dearest Friend' and 'my Dear' (*Elegy XII*), and 'fair Love' (*Elegy XVI*). Even when he uses the term 'mistress', it is as a common noun in almost every case, and not as a term of complimentary address.

In *The Expostulation* Donne begins in an accusatory manner:

To make the doubt clear, that no woman's true,
Was it my fate to prove it strong in you?

Thought I, but one had breathed purest air,
And must she needs be false because she's fair?
Is it your beauty's mark, or of your youth,
Or your perfection, not to study truth?
Or think you heaven is deaf, or hath no eyes?
Or those it hath, smile at your perjuries?

(11. 1-8)

In Jonson's *Elegy XXXVIII*, the poet is the offender; he begs his mistress for forgiveness in the most abject manner and continues unbrokenly from the beginning to the end in the same semi-serious fashion of theological argument. But in *The Expostulation* there is variation: the speaker first reviles the woman for her falsehood—the natural prerogative, he says, of her sex. Even when in the later part of the poem he relents, he still takes no blame to himself, but casts it partly on a third person and partly on the woman's weakness. Thus there begins a long bout of vigorous cursing that goes on till line 52, and at the end the speaker starts making love:

Now have I curst, let us our love revive;
In me the flame has never been more alive;
I could begin again to court and praise,
And in that pleasure lengthen the short days
Of my life's leaf...

(11. 53-57)

The dramatic quality of the elegy is to be found in its representation of the alterations in the lover's mood. This is in vivid contrast with the static mood and rather monotonous entreaties of the speaker in Jonson's *Elegy XXXVIII*. The sharp angry interrogations of the wronged lover in Donne's poem and the fluctuations of his mind set the argument in an actual setting where it comes alive and expresses emotion. Moods change with lightning speed; and 'the moods of a poem by Donne', as Patrick Cruttwell observes, 'are its *dramatis personae*, its plot is their interplay.'[61] The language is made to keep up with the action. In the first part of the poem the lover has no time for analogies and his questions are sharp and straight; but when he relents and feels the need of consoling his woman he backs up his arguments with illustrations:

> Sooner I'll think the Sun will cease to cheer
> The teeming earth, and *that* forget to bear,
> Sooner that rivers will run back, or Thames
> With ribs of Ice in June would bind his streams,
> Or Nature, by whose strength the world endures,
> Would change her course, before you alter yours.
>
> (11. 27-32)

The piling up of so many analogies shows the lover's want of confidence in his protestation of his woman's constancy. On the other hand, the very length and enormity of cursing suggest that it is aimed less against the alleged traitor and more at gratifying the woman. Finally the lover claims that his passion is as strong as ever. The person thus evoked by the poem is a lover of divided identity who can be passionate but has reason enough to consider his feelings with detachment: one who is aware of the actualities of love. Love, he comments at the end, is 'got by *chance*', but 'kept by *art*.'

On his Mistress (*Elegy XVI*) is a poem in which the speaker dissuades his young sweetheart from her wish to accompany him on a foreign journey disguised as a page. In one manuscript alone, the Bridgewater, it is entitled *His wife would have gone as his page*.[62] This has resulted into much controversy whether or not this poem was addressed to Anne More.[63] It is the tender note in the poem which has led critics to such an assumption. However, the point is unimportant to one who is interested in the poem mainly as an artistic achievement. It is the reality of the poem which matters and not whether it refers to an actual incident in the poet's life or an actual woman.

The fact is that *On his Mistress* is a superb piece of drama. It is not merely that the poem is an argument and persuasion —in dialogue form, though that is partly responsible for our response to the poem. There is a logical base and the poem proceeds in distinct stages, from *'profitableness*, to *honesty*, to *possibility*, to *difficulty*, and finally to the persuasive recommendation of a better course to follow.'[64] But to take this structural framework as the end of the poem is to miss its real matrix—its tender human situation; its subtle transitions of mood and yet the unity in complexity which is a characteristic of Donne; its suggestion of a flesh-and-blood presence behind the logic and argumentation; and its smooth and effortless handling of colloquial language. Taken as a whole, what is most important is that the poem is so vivid, like so many other poems of Donne, because it is wholly and clearly dramatised. It presents feelings in action; feelings are not just described. This is the key to the sense of immediacy we feel in *On his Mistress* as also in many other dramatic lyrics of Donne.

The poem works overtly through the situation of a lover persuading his mistress against her determination to go with him on a foreign journey disguised as a page, and there is throughout the poem the speaker's consciousness of other people besides himself. It opens with a typically dramatic rhetorical tirade, with balance and repetitions:

By our first strange and fatal interview,
By all desires which thereof did ensure,
By our long starving hopes, by that remorse
Which my words' masculine persuasive force
Begot in thee, and by the memory
Of hurts, which spies and rivals threatened me,
I calmly beg: But by thy father's wrath,

By all pains, which want and divorcement hath,
I conjure thee, and all the oaths which I
And thou have sworn to seal joint constancy,
Here I unswear, and overswear them thus,
Thou shalt not love by ways so dangerous.

(11. 1-12)

There is a quality of artificiality, of the mock-heroic, about these lines, but the very next lines indicate a change of direction and strike a note of affectionate loyalty:

Temper, o fair Love, love's impetuous rage,
Be my true Mistress still, not my feign'd Page;
I'll go, and, by thy kind leave, leave behind
Thee, only worthy to nurse in my mind,
Thirst to come back; o if thou die before,
My soul from other lands to thee shall soar.

(11. 13-18)

Whereas shifts in mood and tone such as these are a sign of the existence of a real person in a situation which has strongly moved him, his growing perceptions and responses are conveyed by devices of language. The same words are juxtaposed and given contextual variations to gain a new emphasis and to produce dramatic enactments:

Here I *unswear*, and *overswear* them thus

(1.11)

Temper, o fair *Love, love's* impetuous rage

(1.13)

I'll go, and, by thy kind *leave, leave* behind ...

(1.15)

The lover goes on to warn his mistress against the perils of her unwise venture of accompanying him in disguise. Some of his warnings may affect a fastidious reader as being in bad taste, but there is only an unsparing realism about their frankness. If the words lack grace, they have at least greater expressiveness. The language is truncated and made to work in abbreviations, and thus to keep up with the action going on in the lover's mind:

> Dissemble nothing, not a boy, nor change
> Thy body's habit, nor mind's; be not strange
> To thy self only...

(11. 27-29)

'Do not disguise yourself as a boy' is compressed into 'not a boy': a parenthesis, flashing across the mind in mid-sentence and uttered just as it came to the speaker's mind. Here, indeed, is quickness of words matching the quickness of action.

And then comes the conclusion where the lover counsels his mistress to be discreet in her love for him when he is away. She should dream and wish him happiness but not confess by her looks their long-hidden love. She should neither praise nor blame him; nor bless, nor curse openly the virtues of love. Here the lover visualises a nightmare she might have in future. There is a sudden linguistic transformation and a change in the angle of address as the 'Thou' hitherto used in the poem for the mistress is changed to 'I'. The dramatic effect caused by this is further accentuated by a vivid representation of the girl's imagined weird vision and of her frightened outcry in verbs which come out as choked sobs:

> ...nor in bed fright thy Nurse
> With midnight's startings, crying out, oh, oh
> Nurse, o my love is slain, I saw him go

O'r the white Alps alone; I saw him I,
Assail'd, fight, taken, stabbed, bleed, fall, and die.

(11. 50-54)

We have now seen in sufficient detail a good number of Donne's dramatic elegies to be able to reach certain useful conclusions about the dialectical structure of many of them. Such a consideration is demanded by the fact that logic is so constant and vital a feature, not only in the elegies, but in almost all the poems of Donne. This has been explained as an outcome of the infuence of medieval Scholasticism on Donne. Though a dialectical evolution is not infrequent in Elizabethan lyrics and sonnets, there is a more medieval texture in Donne's poems than in the conventional Elizabethan love poems. This is so perhaps because Donne's poems are more dialectical.[65]

Both circumstances and temperament, it seems, were decisive in shaping the structure of Donne's poems into the dialectical form.[66] Donne was early subjected to strict Jesuit instruction which leaned heavily upon the *Summa Theologica* of St. Thomas Aquinas; he attended Oxford and Cambridge at a time when both universities required their scholars to take a five-term course in logic, with frequent lectures and tri-weekly disputations. His training at Lincoln's Inn, his wide reading in Scholastic philosophy and theological casuistry, his experience as a controversialist in the service of Horton, and his membership in King James's little symposia for religious and secular debates further necessitated and effected the development and use of his logical faculties, as did also that long inner debate which preceded his entrance into the ministry. In the period during which Donne's poetic style was being formed and crystallised, he was trained for the composition of prose of comparable logical qualities, e.g., the *Paradoxes and Problems* and *Biathanatos*, both of which are marked by clever sophistry and syllogistic reasoning;

Pseudo-Martyr, 'wherein out of certain Propositions and Gradations, this conclusion is evicted'; and *Ignatius his Conclave*, a dialectical burlesque of dialectic. No wonder, to the subtle mind of Donne, equipped thus by experience and knowledge with the ready and facile weapon of organised logical thought, the use of dialectic came almost as second nature. Logic is so important in Donne's poetry that we could say of it what A.H. Gilbert has said of logic in the drama of the time of Donne—that 'its presence underneath many argumentative and expository passages may be inferred even though its terms and methods are not obvious.'[67]

Whether the contention is that of thought against thought within a man, or mood against mood. Donne makes full use of logical argumentation to develop conflict. The argument in *Love's Progress*, apparently unserious, emphasises the actuality beneath the metaphors and reveals the complexity of the speaker's personality: he may be a rational character or just a man with commonsense, but he is also very much enamoured of hyperboles. The pattern of *Going to Bed is* logical, but it is the logic of feeling, of an individual involved in a real situation, all of which together constitute the dramatic. *The Expostulation* is continually argumentative, but from its arguments we gain a recognition of opposition of moods. The nature of the subject of *On his Mistress*—an argument from *cause*—requires dialectical treatment, but here again dialectic expresses variations of mood or a character in growth,

The Dream illustrates the correlation of the idea and the image, or the intellectual and the dramatic, and what is also significant, the habit of the poet of making his character turn in on himself—as we find in the concluding part of the poem. After asking the 'Image' to depart, the lover counters himself and begs it to stay. This may be explained away with the remark that this kind of reversal is simply the rhetorical device of *epanorthosis*,[68] well-known and widely practised at

124

Donne's time. The best reply to such an approach would be:
'This makes no difference. What matters is the choice of
rhetorical devices and the use to which they are put.'[69] The
device is, in fact, used by Donne not for a rhetorical but a
dramatic end. This self-contradiction is a constant habit of
Donne's mind, and one that applies, among the metaphysical
poets, only to him. It shows itself frequently, either in long
and complex self-arguments, or in smaller and less complicated turns of thought. In other argumentative poets we may
find an interest in the progress and in the processes of
thought, but it is never—as in Donne—the main thing.
Donne is interested in definitions, analyses, and suppositions;
he is little interested in the things into which they issue, even
if in his sermons he forced himself against his natural inclina-
tions.[70] Argument, as Donne's dramatic elegies manifest, is
not concerned with proving ideas in the abstract. In Donne
it has a more sensuous and passionate end, and we may call
it 'an imaginative form of rhetoric.' Donne's arguments are
commonly employed for pointing out or magnifying emotions, and it is not surprising that in the course of this some
ideas are proved. He uses logic for producing effects of
surprise and for exploiting the oppositions of thoughts and
feelings and moods. The rhetoric of emotion in his poems
constantly takes unexpected forms and develops unusual but
not irrational or illogical consequences. The introspection
and analysis we find in his poems turn naturally to reason
and to logic for assistance, but the focus is still on evoking
and dramatising situations between two or more persons.

Such is the dialectic of the elegies which present
a man-woman relationship. These poems have a dramatic
pattern. They are two-person poems and in them
both the persons exist and are at interplay. There are an 'I'
and a 'Thou'. The 'I' speaks directly to 'Thou' and so the
poems are 'I-Thou' poems,[71] records of 'I-Thou' experiences.
It should also be noted that Donne's 'I' is, unlike that in

Shakespeare's early sonnets where the 'I' seems lost in the contemplation of an adored one—at once both remote and superior—if not really superior, at least always on the same plane as 'Thou'. It is the 'I' who discovers the 'Thou':

How blest am I in this discovering thee!
(*Going to Bed*, 1. 30)

But the 'Thou' is vital to the life of the 'I.' The consciousness of the 'I' is lost when 'Thou' is lost. *Love's Progress*. in which the 'I' is in isolation, fails to convey a sense of personality as strongly as the other dramatic elegies where 'I' speaks either directly to 'Thou' or is in close relation to 'Thou'. It is interesting to note that the whole argument of the poem is in relation to a third person, that is, a woman or 'She.' Nonetheless, the changing moods in the poem do succeed in convincing us of the presence of a complex person in it. On the other hand, what we are aware of in the elegies which are primarily witty rather than dramatic is not a 'I-Thou' relationship, nor even of the existence of an 'I', but simply of the writer's wit, his ingenious comparisons, analogies, and arguments.

A study of pronouns in the elegies throws some light on their nature. Words in rhyme position[72] are important in the work of most poets, and no poet can prevent his rhyme-words from at least seeming importance. Therefore, unless we assume Donne to have been incompetent in his use of form, a hardly justifiable assumption, we should follow the guidance provided by his rhyme-words. The persistent echo of the personal pronouns, especially of 'I' and 'Thou', their note intensified by their employment for rhyme, through the lyrics of Donne, is a main cause of one of our responses to his poetry. His love poems, and in a lesser degree even his religious poems, always convey a haunting and inescapable sense of personality, not the details of appearance, behaviour, and character, but of the inner sense of existence as an individual. No poetry more strongly conveys the feeling of the defined individual existence we all sense in saying 'I', and we never sense it in repeating our own names which are rather external signs to others of our characters; it is in using the pronouns that we distinctly imply: 'I am', 'you are', 'he is.'

In the elegies of Donne, 'I' is used as a rhyme word eight times; 'me' fifteen times; 'you', 'thee' and 'thou' nineteen times; 'us' three times; and 'we' three times. Once their notes have been heard in the rhymes, they become increasingly audible within the lines. It is surprising how often the pronouns occur in positions requiring *ictus,* and how easy it becomes, if the rhymes have been carefully followed, to give this *ictus* where prose reading would deny it. However, a distinction is found in the matter of the employment of these pronouns, between the dramatic elegies and those which are mainly witty. The incidence of the pronouns 'I', 'thou', 'you', and 'thee' is greater in the dramatic elegies. On the contrary, they are relatively unimportant in the primarily witty elegies. *The Anagram* employs 'I' only once, but no 'thou' or 'you'— only 'she.' 'I' occurs in *The Comparison*, but it refers to the mistress in the third person only—'my Mistress.' *The Autumnal* uses 'I' twice and 'you' four times, but does not indicate any 'I-Thou' relationship. In *Julia,* Julia is always the third person, never 'thou.' *Variety* has 'I' but no 'thou.' Among these poems, *Change* and *Elegy VI*, though presenting just a series of cleaver analogies, are the more convincing, because their form is that of an 'I' directly addressing a 'Thou.' In effect, finally, it is the dramatic sense which makes all the difference in Donne's poetry; where it is potent his poems are aesthetically effective, but where it is absent or weak his poetry fails and becomes just a *tour de force*.

FOOT-NOTES:

1. John Donne, p. 94. Though not explicit, there is a suggestion here of an ethical consideration. The subjects of Donne's elegies are mostly uncongenial to conventional morality. This has no doubt come in the way of a just evaluation of these poems. The morally reprehensible and the sordid are not a monopoly of only recent literatures. The Renaissance poetics had a place for this kind of thing. According to Sidney, 'That imitation, whereof Poetry is, hath the most conveniency to Nature of all other, in so much that, as *Aristotle* sayeth, those things which in themselves are horrible, as cruel battles, unnatural Monsters, are made in poetical imitation delightful.' "An Apology for Poetry" *Elizabethan Critical Essays*, vol. i, p. 173. It indicates the Renaissance recognition that even actions morally uncongenial could be the basis of poetry.

2. *Four Metaphysical Poets,* Cambridge, 1934, p. 17.

3. *Ibid.,* p. 18. Grierson makes a similar suggestion about Donne's elegies and the more cynical and sensual poems in *Songs and Sonnets.* Of the difference between Ovid and Donne he says : '...the English poet is imitating the Roman, and that... [his] depravity is in part a reflected depravity. In revolt from one convention the young poet is cultivating another, a cynicism and sensuality which is just as little to be taken *au pied de la lettre* as the idealising worship, the anguish and adoration of the sonneteers.' *Donne's Poetical Works,* vol. ii, p. xi.

4. See Paul N. Siegel's "Donne's Paradoxes and Problems", *Philological Quarterly,* xxviii, p. 34.

5. *The Monarch of Wit,* p. 50.

6. *Life and Letters of John Donne,* 1899. vol. ii, p. 215. This view is favoured by J.B. Leishman in his earlier book, *The Metaphysical Poets,* Oxford, 1934, pp. 13-15. Starting with this he builds a whole chain of events which might have actually happened in Donne's life and connects them with some of the elegies and the *Songs and Sonnets.*

7. "John Donne", *Studies in Literature,* Cambridge, 1919, pp. 100-101.

8. See T.S. Eliot, "Donne in Our Time", pp. 9-11. Writing of the essential oneness continuing from Donne's early to later life, Eliot warns against taking too seriously either the early cynicism or the later remorse of Donne.

130

9. *Donne's Poetical Works*, vol. ii, pp, xl-xli.

10. "Donne in Our Time", p. 10.

11. *Donne's Poetical Works*, vol. ii, pp, 61-63.

12. *Ibid.*, p, xxxiv.

13. Pp. 74-79.

14. It was wit as ingenuity which seems to have made the greatest impression on Donne's contemporaries, even when, like Jonson and Drummond, they were poets whose own achievements and ideals were quite different. 'He esteemeth John Donne the first poet in the world in somethings,' Drummond reported of Jonson: 'His verses of the lost chain he hath by heart, and that passage of the Calm, *That dust and feathers do not stir, all was so quiet.*' (*Critical Essays of the Seventeenth Century*, vol. i, p. 212) Drummond himself gave this character of Donne: 'I think, if he would, he might easily be the best Epigrammatist we have found in *English*, of which I have not yet seen any come near the Ancients. Compare Song, Marry and Love, &c. with *Tasso's Stanzas against Beauty;* one shall hardly know who hath the best.' *Ibid.*, vol. i, pp. 216-217.

15. *The Monarch of Wit*, p. 85.

16. Puttenham remarks in *The Art of English Poesy:* '... there were an other sort, who sought the favour of fair Ladies, and coveted to bemoan their states at large and the perplexities of love in a certain piteous verse called Elegy... such among the Latins were Ovid, Tibullus, and Propertius.' *Elizabethan Critical Essays*, vol. li, p. 26. Shakespeare used the word in this sense only : in *As You Like It,* Orlando 'hangs...Elegies on brambles, all (forsooth) deifying the name of "Rosalind" '; in *The Two Gentlemen of Verona*, Proteus explains the gallant manner of wooing:

> After your dire-lamenting Elegies
> Visit by night your Lady's chamber-window...

(III, ii, 11. 82-83)

Nor was Shakespeare alone in connecting the elegy with the amorous Petrarchan sonnets; abundant evidence shows that the wailing cycles of the 1590s impressed their authors as eminently elegiac. In *Astrophel and Stella*, the channel through which the high-tide of Petrarchism flowed into English poetry, Sidney included eleven lyrics not in the sonnet form, but equally amatory and tearful in mood, which he entitled "Songs."

For a detailed account of the various Elizabethan practices of elegy, see John W. Draper, *The Funeral Elegy*, New York University, 1929; R.M. Alden, *Introduction to Poetry*, New York, 1909, p. 68; Gayley and Kurtz, *Methods and Materials of Literary Criticism*, New York, 1920, p. 28; F. W. Weitzmann, "Notes on the Elizabethan Elegie", *PMLA*, vol. i, June, 1935, pp. 435-443.

17. *Elizabethan Sonnets*, ed. Sidney Lee, New York, 1904, vol. ii, pp. 71ff.

18. *Elizabethan Critical Essays*, vol. i, pp. 238, 285.

19. *Ibid.*, p. 249.

20. *The Funeral Elegy*, p. 33.

21. See note 14.

22. *The Monarch of Wit*, pp. 74-79.

23. *Opere*, ed. Rosini, Pisa, 1822, vol. iv, p. 151.

24. See Paul N. Siegel, "Donne's *Poradoxes and Problems*", *Philological Quarterly*, vol. xxviii, 1949, pp. 507-511. Also, J.E. Spingarn's Introduction to *Critical Essays of the Seventeenth Century*, vol. i, pp. xxix-xxx.

25. See note 14.

26. *Donne's Poetical Works*, vol. ii, p. 76.

27. *The Monarch of Wit*, p. 81.

28. "Andrew Marvell", p. 289.

29. *The Use of Poetry and the Use of Criticism*, London, 1945, pp. 28-29, 55-58, 76-81.

30. *Ibid.*, p. 58.

31. *Ibid.*

32. *Ibid.*, p. 57.

33. "The Nature of Metaphysical Poetry", *Collected Essays in Literary Criticism*, London, 1938, pp, 69-88.

34. Eric Thompson is nearer truth in accepting R. W. Church's assertion (in a review of Eliot's Harvard dissertation on F.H. Bradley) —'that the very heart of Eliot's most fundamental belief as an artist is the necessary union of emotion and intellect; of "thisness" and "whatness".' "Dissociation of Sensibility", *Essays in Criticism*, vol. ii, 1952, p. 209.

35. *The Monarch of Wit*, p. 98.

36. *Donne's Poetical Works*, vol. ii, pp. xxxix; also, xxxviii and xl.

37. *The Monarch of Wit*, pp. 53-60, 71-74.

38. *An Elegy upon the death of the Dean of Pauls, Dr. John Donne*, *Donne's Poetical Works*, vol. i, p. 379. 11. 63-68.

39. See R.S. Hillyer's Introduction to *The Complete Poetry and Selected Prose of John Donne*, pp. xvi-xvii; Robin Skelton, "The Poetry

of John Donne", *Elizabethan Poetry*, pp. 203-204; Joan Bennett, *Four Metaphysical Poets*, pp. 14-17.

40. *The Monarch of Wit*, p. 54.

41. *Ibid.*, pp. 72-73,

42. "The Poetry of John Donne", *Elizabethan Poetry*, pp 208-209.

43. J. B. Leishman also indicates an English precedence in Nashe's *Choice of Valentines*, a poem which never got into print, and for which Nashe and the noble patron for whom he wrote it were severly reproved by Hall and other satirists. Cf. *The Monarch of Wit*, pp. 73-74.

44. *Elizabethan and Metaphysical Imagery*, p. 42.

45. *Ibid.*, p. 43.

46. *Conversations* in *Ben Jonson*, ed. Herford and Simpson, Oxford, 1925, vol. i, p. 133.

47. *Elizabethan and Metaphysical Imagery*, p.43.

48. *Ibid.*

49. *Elizabethan Critical Essays*, vol. i, p. 164.

50. Donne's *Elegy* may be compared with Ovid's poem in Dryden's translation of the first three Books of *Amores*.

51. In *The Monarch of Wit* we have a significant paragraph in which J. B. Leishman clarifies the dramatic quality of Donne's poetry by which it is distinguished from Ovid's: 'Donne...is much more dramatic, [continually throwing himself, as it were, into a part, continually imagining new aspects of the triangular situation, and speaking, thinking, and feeling vividly and rapidly as in a play. While Ovid merely describes situations, Donne enacts them : the nature and details of the situation emerge, as it were, incidentally, from an overheard discourse or tirade. Such elegies are essentially dramatic monologues—monologues, that is to say, whose tone is modified by, adapted to, the particular kind of person Donne imagines himself to be addressing.' p. 59.

52. Donne's lines function in the same way as the lines in *Hamlet*, describing by means of a vivid simile the effect of poison on Hamlet's father. I, v, 11. 68-70.

53. "The Dynamic Image in Metaphysical Poetry", *PMLA*, vol. lvii, 1942, pp. 1039-1045.

54. K.W. Gransden, p. 97.

55. *Elizabethan and Metaphysical Imagery*, pp. 54-55.

56. It is the Pauline antithesis of 'milk for babes and meat for grown men.' See Helen Gardner, "John Donne: A Note on Elegie V. 'His Picture' ", *The Modern Language Review*, vol. 39, October

1944, pp. 333-335. Replying to Grierson's objection to the last four lines of the poem, Helen Gardner says that '...it is precisely of *meat*, in the sense of solid food, that Donne is thinking.' She further adds, 'Just as in devotional writers a distinction is made between love of Christ in His Manhood, which is for beginners in love, and love of Christ as God and Man, which is too hard for those newly turned to Him, so Donne's mistress distinguishes between her childish love, which was nursed on his outward fairness, and her full-grown love, which has by practice in loving come to feed on "tougher meat".'

57.   Grierson suggests that the 'Image' is a picture : *Donne's Poetical Works*, vol. ii, p. 76.   He is opposed by E. G. Lewis ("An Interpretation of Donne's 'Elegie—The Dreame' ", *The Modern Language Review*, vol. xxix, October 1934, p. 436) and F. T. Bowers ("An Interpretation of Donne's Tenth Elegy", *Modern Language Notes*, vol. liv, April 1939, pp. 280-282), who favour the latter interpretation.

58.   "An interpretation of Donne's 'Elegie—The Dreame' ", p. 438.

59.   Quoted in Evelyn Simpson's "Jonson and Donne", *The Review of English Studies*, vol. xv, 1939, p. 275.

60.   Also, *Poems of John Donne*, ed. E. K. Chambers, vol. i, p. 241.

61.   *The Shakespearean Moment*, p. 45.

62.   *Donne's Poetical Works*, vol. i, p. 111.

63.   *Ibid.*, vol. ii, p. 86; E. K. Chambers, *Poems of John Donne*, vol. i, p. 241; *The Monarch of Wit*, pp. 67-68.

64.   *Elizabethan and Methaphysical Imagery*, p, 324n.

65.   The *Donne's Poetical Works*, vol. ii, p. xxxviii.

66.   See E. L. Wiggins, "Logic in the Poetry of Donne", *Studies in Philology*, vol. xlii, 1945, pp. 41-60.   Also, Leslie Stephen, "John Donne", *The National Review*, vol. xxxiv, 1899, p. 596.

67.   "Logic in the Elizabethan Drama", *Studies in Philology*, vol. xxxii, 1935, p. 544.

68.   'Epanorthosis, or correction, amends a first thought by altering it to make it stronger or more vehement.' Sister Miriam Joseph, *Shakespeare's Use of the Arts of Language*, New York, 1949, p. 153.

69.   E. M. W. Tillyard, *The Metaphysicals and Milton*, London, 1960, p. 29.

70.   See *ibid.*, pp. 29-32, 38-39. For a more detailed account of this quality of Donne's mind, see James Smith, "On Metaphysical Poetry", pp. 222-239.

71. Francis Berry, *Poets' Grammar,* London, 1958, pp. 86-92.

72. The suggestion is made by Catherine Ing in *Elizabethan Lyrics : A Study in the Development of English Metres and Their Relation to Poetic Effect,* pp. 232-234. See also Helen Gardner's Introduction to *John Donne: The Divine Poems,* Oxford, 1952, pp. xxxi-xxxii.

CHAPTER V

Songs and Sonnets

II

In order to ensure that we do not exaggerate Donne's originality as a poet it is necessary to remember that he did not entirely reject the Elizabethan tradition of love poetry, inherited largely from the Middle Ages, in which the autobiographical was so strictly subservient to the performed convention as hardly to exist.[1] Writing to Sir Robert Carr, Donne remarked :

> I presume you rather try what you can do in me, than what I can do in verse; you know my uttermost when it was best, and even then I did best when I had least truth for my subjects. In this present case there is so much truth as it defeats all Poetry.[2]

The European convention of courtly love was a semi-dramatic system of stylised behaviour and styles prescribed, within which each individual writer produced his own variation. Although Donne repudiated the sentimentality and blantant unreality of Elizabethan sonneteering, he did not forsake it entirely. He kept its way of writing about the experience of love in a half-detached, half-experimental manner. Though there is much psychological realism in him, his interest is general and philosophical, as Shakespeare's was. The concluding lines of

The Second Anniversary —

> Since his [God's] will is, that to posterity,
> Thou should'st for life, and death, a pattern be,
> And that the world should notice have of this,
> The purpose, and th' authority is his;
> Thou art the Proclamation; and I am
> The Trumpet, at whose voice the people came,

> (11. 523-528)

manifest the traditional understanding of the relation of poetic subject to purpose; the accepted conception of the relation of poetry to rhetorical persuasion and the conventional attitude towards the poet. Donne's love poems accurately reflect the Elizabethan mode of thought. His psychological realism is not a matter of the modern scientific interest in individual case-history that leads to naturalism. His concern is with a number of things besides character-presentation—things such as ideas, words, and wit. The speeches in his poems, as also in Shakespeare's plays, are not only for the illustration of character. *Break of day* ends less dramatically than it begins, In Shakespeare also, at least in the earlier plays, do the characters not often parade their (or rather the poet's) ingenuity after crying out what their hearts feel? The mixture is typically Elizabethan. Sometimes wit is there for its own sake, or a wise word. This was a result of the multi-consciousness that was a feature of the Elizabethan age.

Donne is, like his contemporaries, denotative in his use of words and meticulous in details of style. When he speaks of poetry he uses conventional terms, like judgement, invention, and wit—found also in almost all the Elizabethan critics :

To E. of D. with six holy Sonnets

> See Sir, how as the Sun's hot Maculine flame
> Begets strange creatures on Nile's dirty slime,

In me, your fatherly yet lusty Rhyme
(For, these songs are their fruits) have wrought the fame;
But though the engendering force from whence they came
Be strong enough, and nature do admit
Seven to be born at once, I send as yet
But six; they say, the seventh hath still some maim,
I choose your judgement, which the same degree
Doth with her sister, your invention, hold,
As fire these drossy Rhymes to purify,
Or as Elixir, to change them to gold;
You are that alchemist which always had
Wit, whose one spark could make good things of bad.[3]

Besides this, many of the *Songs and Sonnets* deal with traditional themes of love poetry. Love-dream, the subject of *The Dream*, was frequently harped on by sixteenth-century poets.[4] We find it in both Sidney and Shakespeare. The courting poems among the *Songs and Sonnets*, though not many, were certainly, as far as theme is concerned, no original essays in love poetry. The Platonic attitude of identifying the mistress with virtue, which we find in *The Undertaking* and *The Anniversary*, is common in Spenser. Poems like *The Funeral, The Blossom, The Primrose, The Relique, The Damp,* and *Twickenham Garden,* which Grierson designates Petrarchan, are poems of complimentary adoration or complaint and not much different from what the Elizabethan poets had done all along in their sonnets and lyrics. M. Richmond has discovered one of the Renaissance 'stock' lyric themes, that of the unknown or unknowable mistress, in Donne and demonstrated its presence in *Negative Love*.[5] Many of the ideas and images of the *Songs and Sonnets* were the commonplaces of Donne's time. The idea in *The Ecstasy*, for instance. At Donne's time there was nothing strange about the mystical state of *ecstasis*. In *The Garden* Marvell assumes that his contemporary reader is perfectly familiar with the idea when he makes his soul leave his body and perch on a tree like a bird. Merrit Hughes has argued to establish that we owe *The Ecstasy* to the stream of tradition rather than to an original dramatic impulse on Donne's part. To prove this he refers to neo-Platonists like Antoine Heroet, Castiglione, and Benedetto Varchi, who had all spoken, much before Donne, for the flesh as boldly as Donne.[6] Donne's debt to tradition in the poem does not end with this. Reading *The Ecstasy* we are in a world, not of violent change, but of tradition—seeing man as part of the great order which the Middle Ages had succeeded in imposing on the universe, pictured as a chain of being, a set of corresponding and multifariously connected planes, and a dance.[7] The metaphysical ideas employed by Donne similarly come from tradition, and the same could be said of his allusions to various branches of knowledge. The derivative nature of Donne's scholastic and scientific lore cannot be denied.

But along with accepting the presence of traditional matter and the traditional way of subordinating the autobiographical to the performed convention in Donne's love poetry, it must also be recognised that he immensely widened the traditional way, its range of moods, and so of expression. He never broke from the anchor of reality and revived the whole decayed set-up of Elizabethan love poetry with a technique which is essentially dramatic. This was how he met the demands of the new realistic temper emerging in the last years of the sixteenth century.

The Apparition is a nice example of the new realistic mentality that demanded separation of poetry from music. It is not simple and emotional, like the Elizabethan lyric characterised by directness of syntax, smooth development of word order, fluency, copiousness of language, and easy regularity of verse that would cajole the listeners into attention and serve the purposes of music, but complex and intellectual—character-

ised by economy, concentration, realistic force, and personal
sincerity. *The Apparition* is a poem with a complex rhythm
running continuously from the start to the end, evoking situation and a sense of character with great power and convincingness. One has to read it aloud in, as it were, a single
breath. The speaker (a jilted lover in this case), his love for
the woman rendered cold ('my love is spent'), foretells, in a
manner that has the quality of a prophecy, that the woman
herself must come unpitied to that abstention from passion
she has forced on him, her former lover. The setting and
time are effectively suggested and the poet's insistence
through rhyme and stress on the personal pronouns makes
the reader keenly interested in the character of the revengeful
lover as also in the motives of the woman and her new lover.
There could not be a better example of tableaux-drama con-
joined to the purely psychological one and the vividness with
which Donne has represented the motives of three characters
in interaction within the narrow confines of a short lyric.
Even if the situation of *The Apparition* were a borrowed one
and though the poem begins in a narrative fashion, it suggests
definite individuals, a particular situation, and ends in hints
of secret purpose. *The Apparition*, indeed, is an astonishing
achievement.

On the whole the poem expresses a strong personal
emotion, connected intimately with an individual personality.
It has for its subject subtleties and intricacies of emotion,
which require careful and sometimes prolonged expression
and the use of speech sounds governed by feeling. There
are qualities in *The Apparition* which were new to the
English lyrical poetry, though not to drama, in the Elizabethan
period. The facts with which this poem or a poem like
Elegy I deals are ugly; but the ugliness is handled surely and
with unsparing realism. The poetry here does not gloss over
the situation but enforces its crudity. By a peculiar choice
of diction and imagery and through a rhythm that closely

follows the meaning the uniqueness of the situation is emphasised.[8]

Much of the pleasure in reading a poem of this kind arises from the feeling that we are sharing in a private and unusual experience with an identifiable individual. The blending of the inflections of sound and the nuances of meaning—poetry doing what it says—is indeed a dramatic quality. The hard monosyllables—'scorn', 'ghost', 'dead', 'bed'—surrounding the smooth, lingering sibilants of 'solicitation' match the contrast between the man's intention of revenge and the woman's hope that she is free because he is dead. The narrow vowels—'sick', 'pinch', 'wink', 'think', 'shrink'—like the sharp thrusts of a knife, and the snarling rhymes in the last three lines—'spent', 'repent', 'innocent', are examples of the use of word sounds in producing the total effect of the poem. This is no less effective in creating the drama of the poem than the vividness of the picture presented to the eyes— the 'sick taper', the 'cold quicksilver sweat' or the brutal conception of the situation. The cumulative hate of the former lover who expects to die because of his beloved's fickleness and the sheer terror of the woman when confronted by his ghost are successfully reproduced in the long periods which contrast with the strict economy of phrasing :

> When by thy scorn, O murderess, I am dead,
> And that thou thinkst thee free
> From all solicitation from me,
> Then shall my ghost come to thy bed,
> And thee, feign'd vestal, in worse arms shall see;
> Then thy sick taper will begin to wink,
> And he, whose thou art then, being tir'd before,
> Will, if thou stir, or pinch to wake him, think
> Thou call'st for more,
> And in false sleep will from thee shrink,
> And then poor Aspen wretch, neglected thou

Bath'd in a cold quicksilver sweat wilt lie
A verier ghost than I;
What I will say, I will not tell thee now,
Lest that preserve thee; and since my love is spent,
I' had rather thou shouldst painfully repent,
Than by my threatenings rest still innocent.

Much thought has been given to Donne's application to poetry of the formal and syllogistic logic of theological argument and academic debate, and rightly so. There is hardly one poem by Donne of which a clear prose analysis could not be given; in almost each of them there is some kind of argument. But there is also almost always, in the best of Donne, 'a content or substance or experience, passion, feeling, sensibility, or whatever you prefer to call it';[9] and it is always creating in the reader's mind a profound impression that behind it there is 'a rich and wide and sensitive contact with reality...the realities of what life is, and how it is lived',[10] which could not be conveyed by sheer prose analysis, and which is perceptible mainly in and through the progression of thoughts and the rhythms and modulations of the verse, and through the interaction between these and the logical structures.[11] The manner of argument and the manner of speech are the devices by which Donne's dramatic imagination achieves concrete situation, sense of character, and sense of immediacy. The thought and logic part is important. It makes Donne's poems what they are. But no less important is how the development of thought and logic mingles with the emotional to make apprehensible the content or substance of the poem.[12]

The Dream, with its chain of propositions and reasonings, as well as its abstract and intellectual form, is an illustration of the translation of logic into poetry by making these parts of a human situation. In a certain sense, a poem may be logical in form, but in another, perhaps more important sense, it cannot be. That is to say that a poem may make use of logic or of syllogistic reasoning, but the poem itself cannot be logic or syllogism. In other words, where poetry is concerned, logic, though frequently present, is always in a subordinate position, subserving the expression of emotion. *The Dream* is, like Marvell's *To His Coy Mistress*, logically reasoned if looked at from the point of view of the speaker or from that of the lady whom he addresses. But from the point of view of the reader who does not identify himself with either of the personages in the poem, it is something quite different : it is the dramatisation of a situation, in which a lover tries to persuade his lady by means of logical reasoning and metaphysical subtleties and, perhaps, makes the lady laugh secretly at his too intellectual method of seduction. From this second point of view, neither the situation nor its presentation can in any sense be called logical. The poetry here is to be sought, not in the logic, but in the development of the total situation; and, as readers, it is to the total situation that we finally respond. Our apprehension of logic in the poem is only a part of our perception of the situation in which a speaker happens to be speaking in an abstract and intellectual manner. *The Dream* is a dramatic poem: it presents a man addressing an individual, and there is sufficient evidence of their unique identities.

To regard a poem like *The Dream* as a mere intellectual diversion, consisting of only an exercise of wit, is to overlook the important fact that the speaker's pleading, although quite clever, is also earnest enough, because 'he pleads for himself, not before an academic jury of literary connoisseurs, but with the one woman whom he loves for the nonce.'13 The speaker's choice of arguments and manner of presenting them are decided by his intention to make his beloved yield. Thus, though its tone is much refined, *The Dream* with its invective against *'Fear, Shame, Honour'* is similar to *The Damp*, in which the lover exhorts his mistress to 'First kill th' enormous Giant, your *Disdain,*/And let th' enchantress *Honour*, next be slain', and *The Flea*, where the woman is told that by yielding to her lover she would lose just as much honour as the life the flea's death took from her.

Moreover, *The Dream* is dramatic, not only in its presentation of situation and character, but also in terms of structure. It has the structure of the classic Aristotelian plot; it is dramatic in the same way as *Oedipus Rex* or *Hamlet* : a temporal or causal sequence of events with a beginning, a middle, and an end. The scene is a room, lying (as we understand) in semi-darkness, and there is a man resting in it. The woman comes in while he is dreaming of her and sits near him. Her presence wakes him and he thanks her for coming :

> Dear love, for nothing less than thee
> Would I have broke this happy dream,
> It was a theme
> For reason, much too strong for fantasy,
> Therefore thou wakd'st me wisely;...

> (11. 1-5)

Yet, he adds, her coming does not interrupt his dream, but continues it; and he uses the occasion to pay a highly metaphysical tribute to her :

> Thou art so truth, that thoughts of thee suffice
> To make dreams truths; and fables histories;...
> (11. 7-8)

The sensuous part of the lover now emerges and we understand what after all his arguments and tributes have been driving at :

> Enter these arms, for since thou thoughtst it best,
> Not to dream all my dream, let's act the rest.
> (11. 9-10)

In spite of all this gentle entreaty, however, the woman does not come nearer. So the man uses Scholastic theology to lure her forward. As her coming in woke him, he thought her at first sight to be an angel, but when he realised that unlike an angel she could look into his heart and know his thoughts—what he dreamt and when excess of joy would wake him—coming precisely at that moment, he could not but regard it as 'Profane, to think thee any thing but thee.' While we read the second stanza we keep on seeing the lover stretching his arms towards the woman and she smiling enigmatically.

The reversal occurs at the beginning of the third stanza. There is a change in the situation, with the woman rising up, not to draw nearer, but to go away. As her coming in when the lover was dreaming of her had made it 'Profane, to think thee any thing but thee', so now as she prepares to leave he suspects that 'Thou art not thou.' Does she feel, the lover asks himself, ashamed of her conduct in imperilling her honour by coming alone to his room? Is her fear stronger than her love? At last, there is Discovery, of the knowledge that she is a coquette :

> Perchance as torches which must ready be,
> Men light and put out, so thou deal'st with me,
> Thou cam'st to kindle, goest to come; . . .
>
> (11. 27-29)

But this is not really much of a comfort to the craving lover who would fain dream again of her coming or else die of the anguish of unfulfilled desire. The whole poem thus has a causal sequence and a structural form of division as found in drama.

The Dream may be profitably compared with some other love-dream poems, such as Sidney's "Thus night while sleep begins, with heavy wings" and Shakespeare's "When most I

wink, then do mine eyes best see." By such comparative
analysis[14] we may realise to what extent Donne's poem meant
a new departure at his time. The man in his poem, on
waking up, does not address a rhetorical complaint to an
absent or ideal lady. His beloved has actually come to his
room, and the brightness of her eyes, 'As lightning, or a
Taper's light', rouses him from sleep. *The Dream* is conclu-
ded on a note of wistfulness, but even here the contact with
reality may be felt. Being a lover's argument with his
beloved, the poem is not sung but spoken. The passionately
reasoned appeal cannot be fitted into self-contained lines.
Neither can musical cadence express a whole complicated
state of mind. The lines in the opening stanza form but one
sentence. The same is true of the second stanza. There is
hardly a line in the whole poem which makes sense by itself.
The meaning is rounded off only at the end of the poem.
The basic unit in the poem is not the line, but the stanza, or
rather the entire poem. Donne's sole preoccupation is with the
whole effect. Having chosen words with hardly any asso
ciation other than what they derive from the immediate
context, the poet depends on rhythm and intonation to bring
out the experiential element. Each part of the poem is, in
fact, made intensely alive. It is by the interaction between
the speech rhythm and the thought, by giving the right
emphasis to every word and getting the maximum out of them,
by making every word—as it were—heart-felt, that the poet
builds up the excitingly dramatic effect of the poem.

The good-morrow is an instance of the Aristotelian conception of plot in a different way. Here the whole drama takes place
in the speech of the lover, who arrives at the threshold of discovery through the logic of his own conceit. Plot becomes a universal structural pattern largely through its key parts, Reversal and
Discovery, which are by no means limited to broad actions
taking place before an audience and centring round a visible
and moving protagonist ; they may also apply to changes of

feeling or thought or to flashes of insight that occur in the course of a lyric. As a reversal of intention (from the standpoint of a particular character) or a reversal in the direction of the action (from the standpoint of the spectator), *peripeteia* is not identical with a reversal of fortune or situation, according to Aristotle's prescription for tragedy;[15] in a 'simple' plot (*Poetic*, chapter 10), change of fortune may take place without either *peripeteia* or Discovery. In the case of some lyrics in which there is an intense concentration of effect, reversals, of situation, intention, and direction, may be fused in one— along with Discovery, the 'change from ignorance to knowledge';[16] all together, they may constitute the denouement of the highly condensed plot. Thus a pattern of dramatic plot may develop within a lyric frame, with the speaker playing the role of the protagonist whose 'actions' are contained in his words and who is brought to Reversal or Discovery by what he himself says. And this plot may not always govern only external events or relationships, but a subjective, inner experience, which may verge on the mystical or visionary but almost always is concerned with a psychological attitude or state of conciousness to which other circumstances are assimilated.

The three stanzas of the poem are peculiarly appropriate to its dramatic plot. In the first stanza the past is the theme of the lover's speech. This is essential because the love experienced by the lovers at present, to all appearance an earthly phenomenon, must have something preceding it. But the past—before 'we lov'd'—confronted with the present when their souls have been awakened to love cannot be equally important. The past is therefore proved fanciful and childish in its fondness for 'country pleasures' as well as a sort of sleep with its grosser manifestations like snorting.

The second stanza marks the reversal, the change in the situation of the lovers :

And now good morrow to our waking souls,
Which watch not one another out of fear ;
For love, all love of other sights controls,
And makes one little room, an every where.

(11. 8-11)

As James Smith has pointed out, there is now a shift from time to space. The present is now the subject of the lover's discourse, and in the present, while there is no question of a before, there is one of an elsewhere.[17] The lovers, though they are in 'one little room', are themselves the world. Outside that room there is a vigorously active world which explorers are ever expanding with their discoveries of new continents. Yet this active, expanding world, too, like the past merging into the present, is assimilated into the lovers' little room making it 'an every where.'

The idea of the lovers making one world ('Let us possess one world') is carried into the third and last stanza. The situation of the lover speaking, the woman sitting before him looking silently into his eyes, emerges in the very first line : 'My face in thine eye, thine in mine appears.' True plain hearts appear on these faces. This causes the lover to revert to the idea that he and his beloved are two hemispheres (which incidentally explains the contradiction in the second part of line 14 which suggests that each of the lovers is a world, and the implication seems to be that there are *two* worlds, not one) forming one world, an ideal world, the like of which cannot be found anywhere :

Where can we find two better hemispheres,
Without sharp North, without declining West ?

(11. 17-18)

This suddenly causes the revelation that their love is like a simple substance which knows no decay because there is no contradiction between its elements, There is a hint of the time to come in the last lines which express a metaphysical dogma :

> Whatever dies, was not mix'd equally ;
> If our two loves be one, or, thou and I
> Love just alike in all, none of these loves can die.
>
> (11. 19-21)

The idea may be traced back to Aquinas,[18] but the real significance of its presence here is that it is a spontaneous discovery by the lover as a result of the logic of his impassioned monologue. There is no sense of incongruity in the appearance of the idea. In fact, it is the inevitable end towards which the whole poem has been moving. For those who hold the convictions of the first two stanzas the future can have no fear of death or decay. The poem has, as we have seen, a virtually Aristotelian pattern ; its speaker is the protagonist, his speech is the action which moves from the antecedent of the past to the change in the present, and then to the vision of the future.

The theme of *The good-morrow*, the all-sufficiency of love and the image of lovers as a world in and for themselves, is a favourite of Donne, recurring in *The Sun Rising*, where it is given a more witty than passionate form, and in the more tender *A Valediction : forbidding mourning, The Anniversary*, and *The Canonization*.[19] The problem of *The good-morrow* is one of lovers who are two and yet one—most clearly a metaphysical problem. Again, like much metaphysical poetry, this poem depends on a vivid and often elliptical use of the device of metaphor, extended by means of a basic philosophy which links the whole of the created universe into the device, primarily philosophical and not poetical, of analogy. The poem, opening colloquially with a question, proceeds quite naturally on to a comparison, which is only suggested and not elaborated, of the beloved to that Platonic archetype of which all earthly beauties are but dim reflections, and then of her and himself, first to two perfect hemispheres and then to one simple substance—indestructible because irreducible to anything less primary and elemental than it already is. The poem has thus an obviously general and philosophical interest. But it comes out as a particular experience if approached as the contemplation of an idea by a man because it is present for the moment in his mind : he observes his emotion colour it and observes it colour his emotion, and plays with it instead of using it as a plain and simple meaning. This is, according to T. S. Eliot, Donne's typical attitude towards philosophical notions in his poetry, and an idea thus contemplated and observed 'brings often odd or beautiful objects to light, as a deep sea diver inspects the darting and crawling life of the depths.'[20] There is in such an activity evidence of involvement at more than the intellectual or the philosophical level. The speaker's interest in his analogies and the scholastic doctrine with which the poem ends is emotional.

The sense of passionate reality we feel in *The good-morrow* is partly an outcome of, as it has already been said, the lover's curious observation of an idea, which is a kind of creation. Partly it is because of the setting fleetingly suggested by 'one little room', where the lovers are, and because of the situation of two flesh-and-blood human beings acting in relation to each other—so vividly conjured up in the last stanza. But above all the sense of reality here is an outcome of the aggressively personal quality of the speech of the poem. It gives an air of spontaneity —of the lover being in the process of the very gestation of thought. This is not to say that Donne personally felt like this when he wrote the poem. There is a rhetoric of the familiar style quite as much as of the hieratic, and by the time. *The good-morrow* was written Donne had undoubtedly mastered it. *The good-morrow* was as carefully written and revised as any Elizabethan madrigal composed at leisure to a distant mistress.[21] What is meant by the spontaneity of the piece is not that Donne was spontaneous in composing it but rather that he successfully employed the rhetoric of the familiar style in which effects are as studied as in the rhetoric of the hieratic style. The point is that he has in *The good-morrow* succeeded immensely in relating the sense and the speaking voice, as well as in creating the sense of a man speaking while in the very process of thinking.

Phrases such as 'By my troth', 'Thou and I', and 'Let us' emphasise the presence of characters in the poem. The personal involvement of the speaker in the ideas provides the context for the images and conceits, and is expressed through the employment of 'obstructive techniques.'[22] One of Donne's most common and characteristic means for creating the impression of a man in the process of thought is his ability to slow down his rhythms impeded by the very strength of emotion. The opening of *The good-moorrow* is swift and confident, but the flow of the poem is abruptly checked in the fourth line after which we find the lover reassuring himself by reiterating the facts of his earlier outburst :

T'was so ; But this, all pleasures fancies be.

The same technique, this time in the form of a slowing down, appears in the last three lines of the second stanza whose syntax demands an emphatic, deliberate reading, and where the curious construction—

Let sea-discoverers to new worlds have gone,
Let Maps to other, worlds on worlds have shown,
Let us possess one world, each hath one, and is one.

makes us feel that the thoughts of the poem are developing simultaneously with the lover's growing perceptions. This feeling is further strengthened by the repetitions in the last line of the second stanza, each succeeding phrase coming as an afterthought to the preceding one, and appended as an additional sudden perception. The comparison in line 12 also adds to the dramatic force of the whole poem. Having the effect of 'what if...', the line has the force of both a statement—a passionate assertion—and of an equally passionate supposition—a cry of hope. Thus all the elements of this poem, governed by an artfully concealed art—an art that is nothing if not dramatic, are combined to make 'a construction of involvement.'[23]

Coleridge pointed out that in poems where the author thinks, and expects the reader to do so, the sense must be understood in order to ascertain the metre. He also said that 'to read Dryden, Pope. etc., you need only count syllables ; but to read Donne you must measure Time, and discover the time of each word by the sense of Passion.' The metre cannot be separated from the other components of a poem by Donne : It is a part of the fused whole, not something 'superadded.' The very pauses are like pauses between phrases in music ; they are as important as the phrases themselves. Donne must be read with an ear to his silence as well as his articulations, and with an appreciation of his power to' syncopate.

The Relique is yet another poem which would help us to understand Donne's art. Though it deals with love, less seriously than *The good-morrow* and less universally, and says less about man—the ultimate subject of Donne, it reveals the same quality of metre as is found in the more serious, more universal poems like *The Canonization* and *The Ecstasy*. It contains three stanzas, each having eleven lines, of which the first four are octosyllabic or four-footed lines, and the rest of the length and pattern of blank verse (decasyllabic). In reading the first stanza aloud, which is of course the best way of reading Donne's dramatic lyrics in order to grasp their movement as well as sense, the first two lines, broaching the theme with the typical Donnian surprise and boldness, are found to be regular and equal :

> When my grave is broke up again
> Some second ghost to entertain,

but lines 3 and 4—

> (For graves have learn'd that woman-head
> To be to more than one a Bed).

though of the same length as lines 1 and 2, are yet different in quality. They form a parenthesis an indicated by the bracket signs and offer a dig at women's inconstancy. This is an indication that they are to be treated less seriously than line 2. In reading the parenthesis there is a natural lowering and quickening of the voice. The close of the parenthesis serves as a tiny pause before line 5 is read—which is shorter than lines 1-4 by a foot (two syllables), and returns with still greater concreteness and strength to the situation as it was left at line 2 before the mocking little parenthesis had intruded. The closing of the parenthesis gives us an opportunity to pause after line 4 in part compensation for brevity and in preparation for the major recovery of line 5. The shortness of line 5—

> And he that digs it, spies

is, as it were, disguised by the two powerful monosyllabic verbs—'dig' and 'spies', and there is of course no pause between this line and line 6 which is an obvious emotional climax :

> A bracelet of bright hair about the bone.

It is the first full-length line and also the longest line in the whole stanza. The poetical beauty of the alliteration of 'b', the sense of continuing life in the phrase 'bright hair', associated here with something dead ('bone'), combine to create a powerful emotional impact on the reader ; and we cannot but pause here, taking into account the shortness of the next line.   Line 7—

Will he not let'us alone,

hurries us on, dismissing the wonder of the discovery.   The apostrophe between 'let' and 'us' signifies a contraction, so that the two syllables must have the time of only one.   After this line one can broaden out and be slow and deliberate for the rest of the stanza :

And think that there a loving couple lies,
Who thought that this device might be some way
To make their souls, at the last busy day,
Meet at this grave, and make a little stay ?

(11. 8-11)

The 'commentary' in these lines will probably take nearly as long to read as the 'exclamation' of lines 1-7.

A rhythm such as this, apparently off-hand and impromptu, but really built up with much care and conscious labour, does not serve music or hypnotise with regularly recurring beats. Its flexibility is an evidence of personal sincerity and concern for reality.   Donne's rhythms spring from his meanings and are governed by them.   This can easily be missed by careless reading.[24]   Donne controls the pace of his rhythm and the emphasis by which he arrests as well as goads the reader, forcing him to pause here and to rush on there, in the same way as the genius of an actor sways his audience.

II

Underneath the neat argument and controlled wit of *The Canonization* there is a rich and living awareness of what men and women are, and what love between them can be. In a way *The Canonisation* stands alone among all of the *Songs and Sonnets*, for the person addressed in it is a male friend and the considerable variety of feelings in the poem can hardly be comprehended without reference to him. *The Canonisation* is a vigorous glorification of love, but it begins with a voluminous outpouring of exasperation and contempt. The movement of the poem is marked by the gradual warming up of the speaker, proceeding from a half-jestful, half-scornful impatience to an almost ecstatic vision of ideal love and its single-heartedness and peace. So much does the tone (though not the theme) change in the course of the five stanzas of the poem that it appears almost incoherent at first reading. Yet there is unity in the poem, similar to that found in drama, and it reveals itself in relation to the addressed male friend.[25] The brusque style of the opening lines of the poem is explained by the friend's long and persistent pestering of the lover to give up his love (which is the initial situation). After the impatient and ironical outburst in the first two stanzas the lover pauses for a moment as though to conserve his breath, and here the friend must be understood as trying to get another wise word in, in order to appreciate the sudden transition of the lover from satire against his friend to self-glorification. It seems that the friend rebukes the lovers for being stupid like a couple of night moths drawn by light. The tone of the first two stanzas continues at the beginning of the third, but the main thing now and henceforth is the justification of love and even its ennoblement :

Call us what you will we are made such by love ;
Call her one, me another fly,
We're Tapers too, and at our own cost die,
And we in us find the'Eagle and the Dove.
The Phoenix riddle hath more wit
By us, we two being one, are it.

So to one neutral thing both sexes fit,
We die and rise the same, and prove
Mysterious by this love.

(11. 19·27)

After the third stanza the well-wishing friend once more gets
his chance and should now be understood to object pro-
saically, that unless the lover means metaphorical deaths and
recurrections of parting and re-union he is straying away from
the truth: their love may well destroy the lovers, but not call
them back to life, nor even provide them with a living while
they are in this world. In the fourth stanza the lover admits
the hard facts but remains defiant. Henceforth—and there is
no break between the fourth and the fifth stanzas—the objec-
tions against love are so outnumbered by its perfections that
the lovers are canonized, not as saints of the Church but
as embodiments of the Platonic idea :

And thus invoke us; You whom reverend love
Made one another's hermitage;
You, to whom love was peace, that now is rage;
Who did the whole world's soul contract, and drove
Into the glasses of your eyes
(So made such mirrors, and such spies,
That they did all to you epitomize,)
Countries, Towns, Courts: Beg from above
A pattern of your love!

(11. 37-45)

The Canonization expands its concept as it might apply to
love. Canonization necessitates the rejection of worldly
values, explains the opposition between the worldly and the
unworldly, and becomes the idealising metaphor of the poem.

A study of a poem like *The Canonization* indicates what
logic is actually used for in the dramatic lyrics of Donne. The
logic in this poem is less to convince others and more to

reveal the lover—his commitment and determination, his maturity and alertness, in love. John Holloway has tried to bring out the true import of logic, metaphysics, and philosophy in Donne's love poems by setting them against the poems of the nineteenth-century poet Coventry Patmore.[26] In a sense Patmore was a much more philosophical and metaphysical poet than Donne, and, perhaps, this is what caused the trouble. 'Where in Donne the poem is as it were filled with a great volume of genuine experience, in Patmore there is often instead a kind of stridency, the stridency of one self-preoccupied through the preoccupation of his own ideas; and with this, as is usually the case, a kind of hastiness, sketchiness, in the realities, about which the ideas *are* ideas.'[27] The most important contrast between Donne and Patmore is the difference in degree to which their works embody a broad, rich, and sensitive responsiveness to experience. The hyperboles and ingenuities in *The Canonization* bring with themselves a sense of a deep and significant human experience. This is what, in the end, Donne's wit and argument and hyperbole serve to create in the poem.

The Canonization expresses, as dramatic poetry should, the reality of the speaker as also the reality of a situation composed of a fusion, in sympathy or antipathy, of the lovers and the reproachful friend. Its speech is governed by the situation of which it is but a part. Of course, it is so, more or less, in all of Donne's dramatic poems. But another specially good example of close inter-relationship between situation and tone is provided by the Song—"Sweetest love, I do not go." The unity in this poem, like that of *The Canonization*, is hardly perceived without first realising the situation in which the lines are spoken. The tone of both these poems is modified by and adapted to the particular kind of person addressed by the speaker.

"Sweetest love, I do not go" is, in fact, a valediction, although Donne does not choose to call it so. On the other hand it is different from Donne's other *Valediction* poems because of its simplicity and directness of appeal. It does not offer a term of comparison which might detract our attention from the characters and the situation envisaged by the poem. It differs from the other *Valedictions* in so far as it appeals mainly to the heart, not through the medium of a symbol but directly. It also gives more importance to the addressed woman's part. The departing lover really speaks to her, not above her head, and there is here a comparative freedom from indulgence in wit. This peculiarity may be accounted for by the assumption that the song is one of the two poems in the *Songs and Sonnets* (the other is *A Valediction: forbidding mourning*) which, if Walton's testimony is to be trusted, were addressed by Donne to his wife in strictly personal situations.[28] The song was written by Donne, according to Walton, on the occasion of his leaving for Germany when his wife was pregnant and worried. For once, as K.W. Gransden has said, the poet was determined to speak 'in his true person', not as a metaphysical poet but as a husband.[29] Gransden further says: 'It is as if, today, a "modern" poet, writing a special private poem for someone whom he loved and who had no literary pretensions, should feel it to be fitting and natural to slip softly into a form and manner familiar to the non-specialist.'[30]

While the simplicity of the thought and style of the song and its tenderness are beyond question, in saying that it is 'a special private poem' in which the poet speaks 'in his true person', Gransden has drawn a line—though it is not explicit —between those poems of Donne which portray either imagined or borrowed situations and poems which are personal in the sense that they were based on actual events in the poet's life. If nothing else, the style of the song, so unique and isolated in its simplicity of thought and freedom from wit, so different from the voice we have grown accustomed to hear in the other poems of Donne, suggests that here for once he assumes a person which is certainly not his own.

A poem, whether dramatic or lyrical, represents a process of emancipation from the merely personal. While we cannot for certain know the unconscious activity of the poet's mind that preceded the actual composition of the song, let us for a moment accept that the inspiration for the poem was actually provided by the occasion of his leaving for Germany when his wife was with child and in poor health. This must surely have caused Donne much anxiety, both consciously and unconsciously. In that case his worry and depression and sense of guilt at the sight of his suffering wife formed a state of tension from which he could find relief only through contemplation and poetic recreation of the actual feeling. Through the poetic process, the effort of finding the right words and the right form for expressing the reality and of relating emotional and mental experiences, he achieved objectification and a more thorough grasp of the reality. This probably being the case, there cannot be different principles of artistic creation for different poems, such as *A Valediction: forbidding mourning*—dealing with an actual emotional state in the poet's life, and *The Apparition* or *The Dream* or *The Ecstasy*—whose situation is derived from a source other than the poet's life. In both cases, if the creative faculty has really come into play, as it no doubt has in all these poems, the same process is at work: the unconscious activity of the creative mind and the perfecting of the resulting poem by the more conscious use of the poet's critical faculty, working out the personal into the persona. Donne's imaginative perception and recreation of a situation from Horace or a stock theme like that of *The Dream* could fundamentally be, unless there was a deterioration in his regard for the realities of life and human character, in no way different from his perception and artistic recreation of an event in his own life. He perceives situations as drama, as present and immediate reality, and represents them as such. He is both subjective and impersonal: subjective because the feeling of the event or situation which is reproduced in the poem has become an integral part of his imaginative life, and impersonal because of the need for conscious effort and selection and judgement for an artistic achievement of the initially perceived pattern. In both cases, Donne the Poet speaks as directed by the artistics requirement of the situation in hand.

What is really significant when we are considering the song is that Donne perceived the situation reproduced in the poem with an imagination essentially dramatic in its mode and recreated it as drama in certain fundamental essentials. Its simplicity and tenderness are dramatic in the same way as the intellectually tough and dialectically subtle form of poems like *The Dream* or *A Nocturnal* or *The Ecstasy*. Of all these poems the subject is, in a way, Donne himself, and yet in all of them there is the impersonality such as is found more obviously in great drama. As Patrick Cruttwell states, 'Of Donne's love-poetry the true subject is something much more than simply the experiences of John-Donne-in-love; the subject is love itself, situations between persons in love or concerned with love, moods, attitudes, experiences, experiments in love.'[31] This is a proper approach to Donne's love poems and without this the multi-directions in them remain unresolved: their many contradictions, the conflicting attitudes ranging from the scornful lust and aversion of *Elegy I* and the 'sheer blackguardism' of *The Indifferent* to the tenderness of "Sweetest love, I do not go" and *A Valediction: forbidding mourning*, and even Platonic idealism such as is found in *The Canonization, The Anniversary*, and *The Undertaking*, and the stylistic variations and the different voices we seem to hear in them. The patterns we deduce from them are dramatic patterns, arising out of the poet's multiple personality of which he was only too well conscious and which he was incapable of changing even though he repudiated it:

Oh, to vex me, contraries meet in one:
Inconstancy unnaturally hath begot

A constant habit; that when I would not
I change in vows, and in devotions.

(Holy Sonnet XIX, 11. 1-4)

'Contraries meet in one' is not only a description of Donne's personality but also an apt description of his love poetry.

The simplicity of the song is not a sign of any want of detachment on the part of the poet. It is no less artificial and carefully constructed than the more complex of the *Songs and Sonnets*. Its tenderness is only as spontaneous as the feeling of *The good-morrow*. There is here an equal mastery of the rhetoric of the familiar style, minus the abstractness and the intellectual toughness we usually associate with the poetry of Donne. This is to say that Donne successfully used the rhetoric of the familiar style to create the sense of a man speaking, plainly and without any intellectual affectation, to console his wife on the occasion of his going abroad. The whole situation is visualised and presented with wonderful insight: the man starting with a joke in an effort to make his grieving wife smile; his initial failure and feeling of helplessness resulting into expression of sombre despondency at the sight of his wife's redoubling grief; and the final relative success he has in assuaging her grief by entreating her to have pity on him. The subdued and pacified tone of the conclusion of the poem is a sign of the husband's final, though partial, success.

It is clear that we would fail to get the true meaning of the song if we took it just as one of those Elizabethan lyrics which give us, in the words of Rosemond Tuve, 'a rich harvest of maxims, generalities and blanket statements.'[32] Lines such as—

O how feeble is man's power,
That if good fortune fall,
Cannot add another hour,

Nor a lost hour recall!
But come bad chance,
And we join to 'it our strength,
And we teach it art and length,
It self o'r us to 'advance.

(11. 17-24)

are not just a generalised sententious statement. In the
dramatic situation in which they occur they serve the purpose
of expressing the man's helplessness and despair when he
fails to comfort his wife. Nor can—

When thou sigh'st thou sigh'st not wind,
But sigh'st my soul away,
When thou weep'st, unkindly kind,
My life's blood doth decay.

(11. 25-28)

be explained away as just rhetorical persuasion in a general
sense. The lines do persuade, but the persuasion comes
from an individual and is set in a specific human situation
or context.[33] This is not to deny the general and philosophical interest of Donne. He does employ language for
'intimating and ordering significances which particulars
shadow forth',[34] but the ideal, as we have already seen in the
chapter on elegies,[35] can only be approached through the real.
The Renaissance artistic conception of imitating the idea, not
the actual experience, was thus not in conflict with the
dramatic representation of 'facts about a particular *thou* or *I*
in their character of particular phenomenon.'[36]

However, Donne's poetry is dramatic in the way of Elizabethan drama, not in the way of the modern naturalistic
drama. He reconciles the claims of the universal and the
particular, combining narrative with the purely dramatic, and
including many things apart from character in his poetry—

sometimes for their own sake—things like maxims, generalities, and witty statements. But even after admitting all this Rosemond Tuve's comment, that the repetitive and the intellectually pleasing and subtle rhetorical persuasion in—

When thou sigh'st thou sigh'st not wind,
But sigh'st my soul away,
When thou weep'st, unkindly kind,
My life's blood doth decay—

Is aimed at moving the affections and faculties in the reader, appears to be a misreading of the poem. These lines no doubt affect the reader, but as rhetorical persuasion they are addressed not to the reader but to a particular woman in a particular circumstance. It is the whole situation between her and the man speaking to her, two individuals acting and reacting upon each other, of which this persuasion is but a part, to which the reader ultimately responds.

In tone *A Valediction: forbidding mourning* is identical to "Sweetest love, I do not go" and this is why Grierson believes that the two were written at the same time.[37] But, again, the surmise that the *Valediction* is addressed to Donne's wife does not alter the artistic and objective character of the poem.

The successful transmutation of an event of reality into an art-form is found in the wonderful appropriateness of the stanza pattern to the subject of the poem and in the inseparable blending of argument with the emotional substance. At the most obvious level the *Valediction* is a set of propositions supported by argument from analogy. The first three stanzas amplify the main idea: let our parting be peaceful. This is done by means of two similes or analogies. The lover wishes the parting to be as peaceful as the death of virtuous men and as inconspicuous as the supposed trepidation of the crystalline sphere. This is followed by an argument advanced in support of the idea that the love of true lovers is independent of the senses. It is further illustrated by two more analogies. Their two-fold soul, the husband tells his wife, will not be broken by absence, but would be merely expanded by it like gold beaten into leaf. Or, if they have two souls, they are like the two legs of a compass. Thus in *A Valediction: forbidding mourning* parting is related to body and soul. To be demonstrative would profane their love. The movement beginning in death leads into the movements of heaven and earth, and these serve to define earthly and heavenly loves. If the lovers' souls are one, they are superior to separation; if they are two, they may still be united in response. Hence there is no need for mourning.

A Valediction of weeping is a more passionate affair and conjures up a relationship more elaborate and metaphysical than we have found in *A Valediction: forbidding mourning*. Its ingenuity is extraordinary. The lover, faced with the prospect of parting with his mistress or wife, gives vent to his grief with a luxuriant indulgence. He compares his tears to coins which bear the stamp of his mistress, and by this mintage they are worth something:

> For thus they be
> Pregnant of thee;
> Fruits of much grief they are, emblems of more,
> When a tear falls, that thou falst which it bore,
> So thou and I are nothing then, when on a divers shore.

(11. 5-9)

The same vein and the same elliptical use of the device of metaphor (extended by means of a basic philosophy which links all the parts of the universe into a primarily philosophical device) are carried on into the second stanza. There is a quick development of thought by a succession of images apparently unrelated but offered analogously. The tear that before was a coin now becomes a world. It is all very wonderful, the lover tells his mistress, that she creates worlds by merely appearing in his tears, but she will spoil everything if she herself weeps. Their mixed tears will bring another Flood upon this world. Moreover, by weeping the mistress will destroy herself, the lover's Heaven. Thus the picture of the Creation, the Flood, and the destruction of Heaven is completed. 'This world' is, of course, the lover himself. The mistress creates worlds by merely appearing in his tears, but she will destroy him if she weeps herself, and moreover in doing so she will also destroy herself, the lover's heaven and happiness.

This ingenious argument leads quite naturally to the thought of the last stanza, the fine emotional climax and the wonderful touch of whose opening can hardly be fully appreciated without grasping the argument which has gone before:

O more than Moon,
Draw not up seas to drown me in thy sphere.
Weep me not dead, in thine arms, but forbear
To teach the sea, what it may do too soon;...

(11. 19-22)

This is the cry of a lover begging his weeping mistress to spare him destruction while he is lying in her arms, the 'sphere' where they yet have each other, where he feels safe from all dangers, and which is the last place where he would like to feel like a dead man. The wit of the lines accentuates the passion, no less intense than that of the tortured articulation that *The Expiration* is :

So, so, break off this last lamenting kiss,
Which sucks two souls, and vapours Both away,
Turn thou ghost that way, and let me turn this,
And let our selves benight our happiest day.

We ask'd none leave to love; nor will we owe
Any, so cheap a death, as saying, Go.

(11. 1-6)

But, at last, the tone of the lover changes because his passion has exhausted itself. Through an argumentative expression of his grief, dazzling in its wit and quaintness, the lover finally gains relief and calm of mind, and his language in the last two lines of the poem becomes flat :

Since thou and I sigh one another's breath,
Who e'r sighs most, is cruellest, and hastes the
                                        other's death.

(11. 26-27)

The movement of *A Valediction : of weeping* is dramatic in the sense that it presents a character arriving at a proper understanding of his disturbed feelings through a symbolic recreation of those feelings and by a combination of the emotive and the cognitive. This character can talk in the language of high idealism and yet retain frank realism in his immediate rejection of the Platonic ideal that there can be no separation between true loyers; he can be ironic in his attitude towards his mistress even while attributing to her the divine power of creation. Furthermore, *A Valediction : of weeping* is also dramatic in a more specific sense—in the sense of having a tertiary structure, similar to the three-fold structure of the plot of drama. The three stanzas of the poem are specially appropriate to such structure.

In a sense both *A Valediction : forbidding mourning* and *A Valediction of weeping* are poems of abstract ideas, developing by close and precise argument. Yet they are neither coldly logical nor abstract. The argument of both the poems suggests deep feeling. This is because of the sense of individual speakers evoked by these poems. Their true subject

166

is the multiple involvement of individuals and so these poems can affect us as a deeper kind of feeling in spite of their development in argumentative terms.

III

When the feeling-content is either nil or in insignificant because the sense of an individual speaker is not conjured up, even though they are built on the same argumentative principle as that of the dramatic *Valedictions*, we have poems which are more witty than impassioned, and in which structure and pattern are almost everything. Such a poem is *The Will*.

A conceptual structure governs the whole poem which is rightly famous for its logical subtlety and coherence. The first five stanzas are in carefully parallel structure, each with its general indictment coming as a climax after concrete examples of accusation which no doubt reflect a razor-sharp wit. The argument directly leads to the conclusion :

Therefore I'll give no more; But I'll undo
The world by dying; because love dies too.
Then all your beauties will be no more worth
Than gold in Mines, where none doth draw it forth;
And all your graces no more use shall have
Than a Sun dial in a grave.

(11. 46-51)

As soon as the poet has told love that he will undo him by dying and thus put him too in grave, the analogies that prove love's futility quite naturally come from under the earth, 'Mines' and 'a grave.' The image of 'a Sun dial in a grave' has great subtlety of thought, because after the poet is dead, the woman who made his love function cannot get at it, just as the Sun cannot reach a buried sun dial.[38] But with all this *The Will* fails to satisfy as a poem, although it is an excellent diversion. The initial psychological situation, that of a lover's complaint against a frivolous and untrue woman, serves only as a detonator to the logical fireworks which shoot so far away from the single psychological situation of revenge upon love that it may be assumed that the speaker is here only partially involved. The sense of the whole man we feel in the poems which combine concept and logic with richness of meaning, that can arise only from intense feeling and a sense of contact with the realities of human life and character, are missing in *The Will*. Its pattern evokes no four-dimensional observer. The piling up of the accusatory paradoxes through the first five stanzas of the poem is a brilliant achievement in invention, but it also reveals that the intention of the poet here is no different from that in a poem like *The Anagram* or *The Comparison* or *The Bracelet*. Even the conversational tone of the poem, a dramatic element, governed by the poet's argumentative intention, fails to give the sense of a real man and a real experience behind the poem, and we find only the clever poet engaged in an academic exercise or what he himself called 'evaporations' of wit. His interest in *The Will* is confined only to a display of his mental dexterity. It is a poem in essentially the same spirit as we have in the encomias and paradoxes referred to before: a poem primarily witty rather than dramatic, where Donne is mainly concerned with exciting admiration and astonishment by a display of his stupendous ingenuity.

There are some other poems among the *Songs and Sonnets* which may be classified like *The Will*, as merely witty and clever poems about love : poems like *A Jet Ring Sent, A Valediction : of my name, in the window*, and *Witchcraft by a picture*. Very close to these poems are *The Legacy, Love's Deity,* and *Love's exchange.*

There are some other poems, forming a group, which are wit-centred but go beyond the circumference of merely literary exercise. They are *The Funeral, The Blossom, The*

Primrose, The Relique, The Damp, Twickenhman Garden, and *The Undertaking* : supposed to have been written by Donne during his middle years and addressed to either Mrs. Herbert or the Countess of Bedford : in which the poet either celebrates his Platonic affection or else complains that such affection is all the women will give. J. B. Leishman, tarring all the poems of the group with the same brush, describes them as 'wire-drawn, hyperbolical peoms', 'least dramatically convincing and most artificial', which positively demand, 'in order to explain their very existence, the hypothesis that they were inspired by a particular relationship and addressed to a real persons.'[39] While the frivolousness of the logic of these poems and their quality of playfulness are not questioned, no sweeping generalisation about their nature, as made by Leishman, can be valid or tenable. *The Funeral, The Relique, The Blossom,* and *The Primrose* have in common a feeling of playful tenderness, but whereas *The Primrose* is more abstract and conceptual, the other three poems have, notwithstanding their frivolity and artificiality, genuine dramatic effects.

In *The Relique* a lover views himself with amused detachment, and its basic situation of the despoiled grave and the passion of 'A bracelet of bright hair about the bone' (which informs the rest of the poem) bring it alive. These elements in the poem give the underlying reality which marks the poem as truly imaginative. The rhythm of the poem is aimed at creating the effect that the thoughts of the lover are developing simultaneously with his growing perceptions. The angle of address changing from 'thou' in the second stanza to 'she' in the poem's last line indicates the consciousness of two persons and in this is truly dramatic. *The Funeral* talks of the distant 'she' throughout, with a dignified melancholy restraint, till, in the last line, view point and mood both change to nearness ('you') and personal bitterness :

That since you would save none of me,
    I bury some of you.

The effect of the poem is certainly very different from what a prose analysis might make one expect and it is anything but 'wire-drawn' and 'hyperbolical.'

The Blossom, a dialogue between the divided parts of a single mind, is a felicitous expression of Donne's self centredness and his habit of regarding what Thomas Browne has called in his *Religio Medici* 'my self;...the Microcosm of my own frame' : the world of his own mind. In its adoption of the dramatic device of dialogue to represent a mind divided within itself *The Blossom* is similar to Yeats's *Dialogue of Self and Soul,* although it ought to be admitted that the debate in Yeats's poem is of a profounder kind and enters into new depths of being and the sublime. Besides this, Donne's dramatisation of the situation in his poem is Elizabethan in character and not so complete as in Yeats's poem. *The Blossom* represents the situation of a dispute between a lover's wisdom, that tells him to go to London where there is an accommodating lady who will respond to his love both physically and mentally, and his perverse heart, 'subtle to plague thy self', which insists on living under the foolish delusion that it may succeed with the cold and repelling lady whom it has been courting in the countryside. The speakers in *The Blossom* are naturally without identity and narration is combined with drama. The speech of the heart is introduced indirectly, in the poet's or the lover's words :

> But thou which lov'st to be
> Subtle to plague thy self, wilt say,
> Alas, if you must go, what's that to me ?
> Here lies my business, and here I will stay :
> You go to friends, whose love and means present
> Various content
> To your eyes, ears, and tongue, and every part.
> If then your body go, what need you a heart ?
>
> (11. 17-24)

But these differences of level do not make the poem any the less dramatic. The wonderful variety of the poem—its smoothly lyrical and beautiful opening, like that of conventional Elizabethan lyrics, but which may yet be subtly ironical against the hopeless adoration of the Petrarchan heart, the retort of the heart which is surprisingly not in the lyrical vein of the opening stanza, and its speech rhythm so close to that normal to Donne's argumentation (it may be a parody of the colloquial idiom that Donne habitually adopts), and finally the scoffing at the heart, and the taunting advice offered to it—conveys first an unwillingness to face the facts of love and subsequently the truth that a man, notwithstanding his love, may exercise his mental faculties in a normal way. It is these glimpses of the varying but all the time real nature of love that give *The Blossom, The Funeral,* and *The Relique* that dramatic convincingness which J. B. Leishman misses in the entire group.

On the other hand, *Twickenham Garden* is a poem, which begins with a fierce absorption in passion running through the first two stanzas, but dissipates its dramatic possibilities in the pursuit of wit and paradox—which have no emotional function—in the third and last stanza :

> Hither with crystal vials, lovers come,
> And take my tears, which are love's wine,
> And try your mistress's Tears at home,
> For all are false, that taste not just like mine;
> Alas, hearts do not in eyes shine,
> Nor can you more judge woman's thoughts by tears,
> Than by her shadow, what she wears.
> O perverse sex, where none is true but she,
> Who's therefore true, because her truth kills me.
>
> (11. 19-27)

Here clearly is an example of a failure of Donne's dramatic vision. The symbolic representation (it may be called analogical wit) of the lady's relation to the poet through the mataphor of her garden's effect on him, in the first two stanzas, is not sustained. These stanzas evoke a situation and a character and a sense of passionate hostility arising, as it were, from a rebuff against an attempt by the lover to sexualise a Platonic relationship. The unsatisfactoriness of the third stanza is not only a matter of violation of good taste felt in the uncongenial and grotesque image of the poet's offer to lovers to taste his tears and then to taste their mistresses' tears to ascertain how faithful they are. A false note pervades the whole of the last stanza; its hyperbolical statements, its ambiguity, and its paradox mark a degeneration of the dramatic substance of the first two stanzas into a mere striving after clever effects. Thus *Twickenham Garden* finally turns out to be just a *tour de force*, perhaps attempted by the poet to impress his patroness.[40]

It would be useful to make a comparison of *Twickenham Garden* with *A Nocturnal upon S. Lucy's day, Being the shortest day*. The title of the poem, *A Nocturnal upon S. Lucy's day* (and Lucy was the name of Lady Bedford) and the similarities of the poem in thought, feeling, and rhythm to *Twickenham Garden* lead one to conjecture that the *Nocturnal* was written, like the other poem, to the Countess of Bedford, and the occasion usually associated with the poem is supposed to be the dangerous illness from which the Countess recovered in 1612.[41] Doniphan Louthan, though connecting the *Nocturnal* with Lady Bedford, makes an unusual interpretation.[42] He believes that the poem was written on the occasion of Lucy Harington's marriage to Edward Rusell, third Earl of Bedford, on December 12, 1594, an event which left Donne in a profound depression of spirits.[43] But however we regard the poem, whether it was inspired by Lucy's serious illness or her marriage, the difficulty felt is whether so sincere a strain as we have in the *Nocturnal* could have resulted from the kind of relation Donne had—we believe—with the

172

Countess. There could be no deep friendship between the two and at most the relation between them was that between a protege and a patroness, not intimate and as between equals.[44] It may be argued from this that it was improbable for Donne to have addressed the *Nocturnal* to the Countess either after her marriage in 1594 (perhaps Donne did not even know her then) or during her illness in 1612. So the *Nocturnal* has been explained as an 'anticipatory elegy' by Donne upon his wife; an attempt by the poet to imagine the nothingness of life without her. If this is accepted, the death of the address-ed lady in the poem is assumed, not actual.[45]

In fact, the only solution to the enigma of the *Nocturnal* is assessing it from the criterion raised in this study : that the most important factors in poetry are imaginative perception of a feeling arising from a situation and successful expression of that perception. The impulse for a poem comes from an event of reality which does not mean necessarily an event in the poet's life. The event may come to the poet's conscious-ness from reading, from observation, from sources external to his own self; but the vitality of the poem, the feeling that here we are witnessing something real and life-like, arises from the poet's creative perception of the event and effective symbolic recreation of the feeling of the event. Assuming that *Twick-enham Garden* and the *Nocturnal* were inspired by a similar feeling, the conventional Petrarchan feeling of a poet for his patroness, and considering the other similarities between the poems such as their intense and brooding atmosphere, their expression of a strong feeling through a complex web of dialectic and rhythm, and their impatient wit, one still finds the *Nocturnal* very different from *Twickenhan Garden*. And the difference is not just a matter of the greater sincerity and profoundness of the *Nocturnal*. The *Nocturnal* produces an effect of greater dramatic reality than *Twickenham Garden*, and this quality, I submit, comes not from an actual event as such, but from the Poet's creativeness, in both perception and expression. Of course, experience in a wider sense is a necessity for the poet, but it is not necessary that there must be an actual, particular experience behind every poem worth its name. The essential difference between *Twickenham Garden* and the *Nocturnal* should be sought, not in how close the actual events behind them were to the poet's own life, but in his creative response to the events embodied in the poems. The dramatic possibilities of the situation portrayed in the first two stanzas of *Twickenham Garden* peter out in the last stanza, but the vivid drama of the *Nocturnal*, the drama of a man caught in a whirlpool of despair and feeling of nothingness, finds consistent and full realisation throughout the poem.

When the over-all pattern of the *Nocturnal* has emerged from its dialectical framework, and from the structure of its total expression which includes, not only the subtle thoughts of the poem, but its images, of a dying sun. of the hydroptic earth which has drunk the general balm, of a complicated and mysterious alchemical experiment, of floods and chaoses, and finally of the vigil in the dark, silent night, and the tones of a speaking voice, it is seen to be a dramatic pattern illustrating the disinterestedness which the poet achieves in the process of transferring an event from the sphere of actuality to the sphere of art. Assuming that the poem is about the death of a mistress, the initial situation of the poem is this death and the consequent feeling of the lover that the world has stopped with her death :

'Tis the year's midnight, and it is the day's,
Lucy's, who scarce seven hours herself unmasks,
The Sun is spent, and now his flasks
Send forth light squibs, no constant rays;
The world's whole sap is sunk :
The general balm th' hydroptic earth hath drunk,
Whither, as to the bed's-feet, life is shrunk,

Dead and enterr'd; yet all these seem to laugh,
Compar'd with me, who am their Epitaph.

(11. 1-9)

But the means by which this bitter despair—the feeling that all vital energy in the world has been sapped—finds expression indicate a hope of resolution in the future. The poet connects the despair with the symbols of the longest nights and of conditions of temporary decline in nature; and as even the longest night is bound to be followed by day and nature must revive and renew itself after winter, the lover's present despair too will ultimately give way to hope and a new life.[46]

This realisation is certainly not remarkable for any startling originality to thought. But it is a sign of a character hovering between two view points—of death and cessation within himself and of the continuance of life without. This character Is lyrical and subjective, but he also has the power of distinguishing between things as they really are and as they appear to him in his grief and hopelessness. Emotional power is behind the first, but the character who has been conceived with dramatic dynamism cannot ignore the evidence of things outside himself. The *Nocturnal* is dramatic in so far as it shows an awareness of both present feelings and those that will come into being later. This kind of awareness is a proof that the experience of the poem is a really felt problem, not just a logical-pedantic riddle in which some odd resemblance is proposed between things quite unlike.

Of course, in a poem such as the *Nocturnal* the anchor of reality is the primary thing. The passion which is the subject of Donne's love poems is neither ideal nor conventional, but love as an actual, immediate experience in all its variety. Even in the apparently most flippant of the *Songs and Sonnets*, where the poet appears to speak without any seriousness whatsoever, there is a note of sincerity, of contact with real life, for the poses Donne adopts in them are not someone else's but his own. Even his witty paradoxes pulsate with the implications of a real situation and are presented with dramatic vividness. In *The Indifferent*, the paradoxes are meant to test, to challenge, and to discover weakness—certainly to be provocative. The speaker develops his indifference to a whole series of opposites that might be expected to limit love, but discovers only one opposite to which he is not indifferent, and that is constancy. This new heresy in love, of which Venus had not heard before, is to be punished by making its few victims true to a false love. So *The Indifferent* breaks the stereotype of Petrarchan love, and indeed suggests, despite all its wit, that no stereotype can limit or confine love. The same realistic trend may be observed in *The Sun Rising*. It has a situation and a feeling similar to that of *The good-morrow*. The lover addresses the sun and his railings sound more rhetorical than dramatic. Yet the scenery, sketched with a few skilful strokes, redeems the piece from the fault of ranting in cold blood : the sunrays peer through windows and drawn curtains into the bed, a property only alluded to in *Break of day*, but here brazenly mentioned in the concluding lines of the last two stanzas so as to leave us in no doubt about its paramount importance. The poem is a successful fusion of wit and passion. The truth that is projected by the poem is this. It is not merely a rhetorical protest against the short duration of the pleasure of love. The lover of *The Sun Rising* is so confident of his liberation from all natural bounds that he dares upbraid the sun, the very source and sustainer of all physical life. The lovers who have enternity in their eyes and on their lips can afford to scoff at the 'rags of time.' Yet it is a physical experience which has brought them to this transcendental condition. The lover seems to be reflecting upon this paradox at the beginning of the second stanza when he plays with the fancy that man is greater than external nature, which can be said to exist only in so far as it is perceived by his senses.[47]

On the other hand, this realism necessitates a special use of language. Whereas the writers of Elizabethan sonnets, mythological idylls, and heroical epistles are content to adorn a conventional sentiment with mythological fancies, verbal conceits, and hypnotic regular rhythms ; Donne returns to the idioms and rhythms of speech—using words, which form conversational diction, not for their own sake but to communicate his consciousness of love, that wonderful phenomenon of man-woman relationship, in all its varying and conflicting aspects, and rhythms, which approximate poetry to the spoken word and are truly dramatic, giving the illusion of immediacy and of someone talking in a state of heightened feeling.

Denne's style refers to his attitude to experience. His realism and intellectual bias make him prefer words which appeal to and activise the mind, rather than those that appeal to the senses and evoke an emotional response through memory. Commonly, the reverberations, or overtones, of words in poetry depend very largely on the memory of sense-impressions they call up, or else the memory of emotions that the same words have evoked in other contexts. Donne neglects this accumulated treasure and if he evokes memories they are of things from science or medicine or law or navigation or philosophy rather than from sense-impression or poetry. We realise that his words have more than their normal prose meaning—they expand and echo as surely as the words of Shakespeare—but they stimulate, not directly the senses or emotion, but the mind. Words consecrated to poetry are avoided because such words have accumulated emotion. The very reasons that prompt other poets to go for such words persuade Donne to reject them. Like Wordsworth in many of his poems he prefers words in everyday use. He uses the language of men when they are soberly engaged in commerce or scientific speculation, so that the words, apart from their sense in the context, have no extra meaning. He cuts himself off from one of the common sources of poetry and thus becomes entirely dependent on a successful balancing between thought and feeling.

Characteristic of the *Songs and Sonnets* is the marked absence in them of mythological or pastoral imagery and allusion. It was, no doubt, partly to this feature that Carew referred in his elegy on Donne.[48] This disregard of mythological or pastoral elements, and of stereotyped poetic expressions, implies in the *Songs and Sonnets* a reaction against conventional remoteness and gallantry. In their place the colloquial nature and tone of Donne's language, as well as his frequent references to war and military affairs, death, law, politics, medicine, fire and heat, business, the human body, and many details of domestic life, establish a firm and even stern realism ; while, on the other hand, an intellectual strain, varying in loftiness, is created by references to Scholastic doctrines, astronomy, religion, learning alchemy and astrology.

The matter of fitting poetry to non-literary diction and the speaking voice has constituted one of the most difficult problems of literary creation at all times. Some obvious rhetorical facts are that there should always be some distinction between the rhythms and the diction of verse and of vulgar speech and, secondly, that there should be a relation between the two and that the relation should be constantly altered and modified in order to infuse new vigour and life into literature. This is, as E.M.W. Tillyard has remarked, a much sounder proposition than the assertion that literature ought or ought not to be close to or distant from the spoken language.[49]

Donne's innovation of the language and style of lyric verse can be best understood in relation to his broad and rich and sensitive responsiveness to experience which is 'the right starting point for an account of how and why Donne himself was great.'[50] This attitude to experience was an outcome of the changing intellectual climate of Donne's time and it led to the introduction of 'a natural conversational diction instead of a conventional one', and of 'the natural or conversational style which the Elizabethans at their best had excelled in producing in a highly sophisticated metric of blank verse,'[51] into lyric. This was also an outcome of Donne's concerns for reality. He broke away from the amplifications and the elaborate rhetorical schemes of the Elizabethans because they were unsuitable to his realism—to his purpose of the hinting and adumbration of the infinite quality of the passion of love, 'the ups-and-downs, the ins-and-outs of human temperament, the alternations not merely of passion and satiety, but of passion and laughter, of passion and melancholy reflection, of passion earthly enough and spiritual rapture almost heavenly,' which are the subjects of his *Elegies* and *Songs and Sonnets*, and for which he is described as 'the inspired political creator.'[52]

Very little of Donne's poetry is descriptive and there is almost nothing in him of the feeling for nature of the Elizabethans, or of their pastoral and ideal pictures of meadow and wood and stream. It would be hard to think of a greater contrast than between Marlowes *Come live with me* and Donne's parody imitation *The Bait*. The subjects and the dramatic form Donne ordinarily chooses in his lyrics do not admit of a slow movement and faithful sensuous elaboration, of copiousness and elaborate word-schemes. Not that he was incapable of description. When occasionally his purpose is descriptive he gives us *Storm* and *Calm*. Amplification and ornamentation might have been sufficient for Donne if his purpose had been merely to praise a lady's physical beauties, or to make elaborate and beautiful illumination of philosophical ideas. In *The good-morrow*, the choice and arrangement of words is simple and direct and felicitous. The poem is in one respect similar to Spenser's "Garden of Adonis" in *The Fairy Queen*. Both make use of philosophy. But whereas philosophy is *the* subject of Spenser and he beautifully and elaborately illustrates it, Donne's subject is love and he uses philosophy as only a support. There is seen by this comparison a sharp difference of intention and correspondingly a difference in result. Spenser's leisurely pace and abundance of pretty sensuous particulars and ornaments do not suit Donne's purpose of recording an immediate passion as unfolded in a situation.

We reach similar conclusions if we compare another of Donne's *Songs and Sonnets,* namely, *The Sun Rising,* with Spenser's *Amoretti No. XV.* Spenser's poem begins with a varient of the image Donne has used in *The Sun Rising.* Why look in 'both the Indias' for riches ? They are all here in my love. But Spenser goes on to make a tiresomely long list of the cargoes merchants bring, and this is very different from the concentration of Donne's *The Sun Rising.* There is again the characteristic difference in diction between the two. *The Sun Rising* is a fine illustration of Donne's contempt for the elegances of poetic diction. The sun, which Spenser and other Elizabethan poets had so often described as 'the golden eye of heaven,' 'Hyperion', and 'the glorious planet Sol', is reduced by Donne to a 'Busy old fool' and 'Saucy pedantic wretch.' However, the bareness and the con.mon-life-diction of poems such as *The good-morrow* and *The Sun Rising* are not incompatible with magnificence. The absolutely colloquial diction and the subordination, as in dramatic verse, of verse pattern and metrical accent to the giving of maximum emphasis and intensity to a natural speech rhythm can create, on the one hand, a poem like "Go, and catch a failing star"— more witty than impassioned, where the experiential or emotive content is almost nil ; and on the other, a poem like *The good-morrow,* which is a successful expression of the awakening of two souls effected by love, not in spite of its seemingly unpoetic language like 'were we not wean'd till then,' 'suck'd on country pleasures,' 'snorted we in the seven sleepers' den,' or its images drawn from sea-exploration and geography, but with them and on account of them. In *The Sun*

Rising, Donne has combined with the impudently contemptuous diction and conversational tone the undoubtedly serious and tender theme of the all-sufficiency of true lovers. The defiantly colloquial diction, partly an outcome of reaction against Spenserian and Petrarchan conventions, becomes an effective tool for the expression of Donne's dramatic imagination. There is a structural unity in *The Sun Rising* which includes all its elements, its impudent address, its ingenious conceit that the sun travels farther only to fare worse, and its more deeply felt, less merely witty and ingenious, idea that the lover and his beloved are a world in and for themselves.

A notable feature of Donne's *Songs and Sonnets* is their rather peculiar sensory atmosphere. They contain very little colour, though there are sometimes remarkably violent exceptions such as we find in *The Flea.* From time to time there are remarkably sharp, colourless visual impressions. But even these are rare, and the focus of attention is very rarely on the visual aspect of experience. What is usually presented in the *Songs and Sonnets* is not a visual impression, but such thoughts and reactions as a visual experience might have aroused in the lover.

The language of *Break of day* is simple and unadorned—naked, in fact, but its very nakedness speaks passion :

'Tis true, 'tis day ; what though it be ?
O wilt thou, therefore rise from me ?
Why should we rise, because 'tis light ?
Did we lie down, because 'twas night ?
Love which in spite of darkness brought us hither,
Should in despite of light keep us together.

Light hath no tongue, but is all eye ;
If it could speak as well as spy,
This were the worst, that it could say,
That being well, I fain would stay,
And that I lov'd my heart and honour so,

That I would not from him, that had them, go.

Must business thee from hence remove ?
Oh, that's the worst disease of love,
The poor, the foul, the false, love can,
Admit, but not the busied man.
He which hath business, and makes love, doth do
Such wrong, as when a married man doth woo.

The poem ends with a couplet of epigrammatic wit, but its feeling cannot be questioned. Here for once, in the *Songs and Sonnets*, the woman speaks, and so well, that this piece alone would suffice to prove Donne's ability to express the feelings of others and convince us that even when the speaker in his love poems is a man he need not necessarily be the poet himself.[53] The feeling of the woman whose lover is about to rise and go away finds utterance in her impassioned address and short, panting questions, following one another in quick succession. Even the woman's exasperation against that bodyless adversary—'business'—sounds natural and sincere in its exaggeration. Visual imagery, amplification, and words with rich literary association would only hamper the simple drama such as we find in *Break of day*.

The dramatic intention of Donne governs his references and choice of diction. While on the one hand the *Songs and Sonnets* have very little of visual impression and colour, they have, on the other hand, a high incidence of words denoting motion. Vivid and rapid enactment of a situation requires words conveying movement and action. It is really surprising to discover the large number of words in the *Songs and Sonnets* which Donne uses to convey these.

A diction such as this concentrates all the time on action (of course, more inner and less external in Donne). The frequency with which the personal pronounce 'I', 'thou', and 'we' are heard in the *Songs and Sonnets* conveys strongly the sense of the existence of defined individuals or characters in clear situations. Such words as 'now', 'here', and 'this' give a sense of immediacy—of an experience in making—as drama does.

FOOT NOTES

1. Arguing against the charge that poets are liars, Sidney holds in his *Apology* that since poets make no claim for the truth of their verses they cannot be guilty of being falsifiers.
2. *An hymn to the Saints, and to Marquesse Hamylton, Donne's Poetical Works,* vol. i, p. 288.
3. *Donne's Poetical Works,* vol. i, p. 317.
4. See Mario Praz, "Donne's Relation to the Poetry of His Time", *A Garland for John Donne,* p. 53.
5. H.M. Richmond, "The Intangible Mistress", *Modern Philology* vol. lvi, May 1959, pp. 217-223.
6. Merrit Y. Hughes, "The Lineage of 'The Extasie' '', *The Modern Language, Review,* vol. xxvii, January 1932, pp. 2-5.
7. See E.M.W. Tillyard, *The Metaphysicals and Milton,* pp. 79-82.
8. While J.E.V. Crofts's assertion that Donne was obsessed with his own self and that he could write only about this (p. 133) is hardly acceptable in view of the dramatic nature of Donne'e love poems, he develops this initial remark into a suggestion which partly explains the powerful fascination exerted by Donne's lyrics: 'Just because he [Donne] is so conscious of himself we are aware of him—the man speaking...every line seems to bear the stamp of his peculiar personality.' "John Donne", *Essays and Studies,* vol. xxii, 1937, pp. 134-135.
9. *The Monarch of Wit,* p. 222.
10. John Holloway, "Patmore, Donne and the 'Wit of Love', *The Chartered Mirror,* pp. 58-61.
11. F.P. Wilson refers to this 'follow-through of logic and passion', found in George Herbert and Marvell, as the sign that they belong to the school of Donne. *Elizabethan and Jacobean,* p. 58.
12. C.S. Lewis, *English Literature in the Sixteenth Century,* Oxford, 1954, pp. 548-549.
13. "The Dramatic Element in Donne's Poetry", p. 46.

14. "Donne's Relation to the Poetry of His Time", pp. 53-57.

15. For these distinctions, see Humphry House, *Aristotle's Poetics : A Course of Eight Lectures*, rev. ed., London, 1956, pp. 96-97.

16. As Humphry House has pointed out (*ibid.*, p. 98), 'Discovery' is not limited to the recognition of objects or persons but is intended to include the discovery of whole areas of circumstance, whole states of affairs, about which there was previous ignorance and mistake.

17. On Metaphysical Poetry", pp. 229-230.

18. Grierson's notes on this have a quotation from Aquinas and a summary of the Scholastic doctrine of the soul. *Donne's Poetical Works*, vol. ii, p. 11.

19. The image of lovers forming a world in and for themselves is common to three of these poems: *The Sun Rising*, ll. 27-30 ; *The Anniversary*, ll. 23-26 ; *The Canonization*, ll. 40-44.

20. "Donne in Our Time", pp. 11-12.

21. See Grierson's various readings of the manuscripts and editions. Donne's Poetical Works, vol. ii, pp. 10-11.

22. Robin Skelton, "The Poetry of John Donne", p. 213.

23. *Ibid.*, p. 213.

24. *Four Metaphysical Poets*, p. 44.

25. The suggestion is made by Pierre Legouis in 'The Dramatic Element in Donne's Poetry", p. 46.

26. "Patmore, Donne, and the 'Wit of Love' ". pp. 58-61.

27. *Ibid.*, p. 61.

28. *Donne's Poetical Works*, vol. ii, p. xxxx.

29. *John Donne*, p. 68.

30. *Ibid.*, p. 69.

31. *The Shakespearean Moment*, p. 46.

32. *Elizabethan and Metaphysical Imagery*, p. 18. Also, p. 21.

33. *Ibid.*, pp. 178-186.

34. *Ibid.*, p. 179.

35. See the chapter on *Elegies*.

36. *Elizabethan and Metaphysical Imagery*, p. 179. See S.L. Bethell, *Shakespeare and the Popular Dramatic Tradition*, London, 1944, pp. 62-81.

37. *Donne's Poetical Works*, vol, ii, p. xxxx.

38. This interpretation has been taken from *Elizabethan and Metaphysical Imagery*, pp. 170-171.

39. *The Monarch of Wit*, pp. 162-163.

40. Twickenham Park was the residence of Donne's patroness, the Countess of Bedford, from 1608 to 1618, and *Twickenham Garden* was almost certainly addressed to her.

41. For a discussion of the problem, See Grierson, *Donne's Poetical Works*, vol. ii, pp. xxii-xxiii.

42. *The Poetry of John Donne : A Study in Explication*, New York, 1951, p. 193.

43. In [her review of Louthan's book, Helen Gardner finds the conjecture attractive because the whole tone of the poem is, to her mind, better suited to a lament upon the marriage of the beloved to another than it is to a dangerous illness of the loved one, *Modern Philology*, vol. i, May 1953, p. 278.

44. P. Thompson, "John Donne and the Countess of Bedford", *The Modern Language Review*, vol. xlix, July 1949, pp. 327-340.

45. *The Monarch of Wit*, p, 198.

46. Richard Sleight has indicated that the symbols chosen by Donne for disillusion, emptiness, and death are year, night, world— 'things in which death is only a temporary state.' This is a definite evidence of his knowledge, even at a moment when life and world have no meaning for him, that life and world will go on. "John Donne : *A Nocturnal upon S. Lucies day, Being the shortest day*", Interpretations, ed. John Wain, London, 1955, pp, 38-39.

47. M.M. Mahood, *Poetry and Humanism*, London, 1950, pp. 97-98.

48. *Donne's Poetical Works*, vol. i, pp. 378-379.

49. *Metaphysicals and Milton*, p. 46.

50. John Holloway, p. 61.

51. "Donne in Our Time", pp. 13-14.

52. G. G. Saintsbury, Introduction to *Poems of John Donne*, ed. E.K. Chambers, pp. xxxii-xxxiii.

53. Joan Bennet : 'If he [Donne] could imagine himself into the woman's part, he could no doubt also imagine himself into other situations which had no counterpart in real life. There is no need then to suppose that every poem had its corresponding anecdote ; if *The Break of Day* is the fruit of dramatic invention, so, may be are the realistic details of some other poems,' *Four Metaphysical Poets*, pp. 20-21.

A SELECT BIBLIOGRAPHY

Allen, D.C., *Image and Meaning : Metaphoric Traditions in Renaissance Poetry*, 1960, Baltimore : The John Hopkins Press.

Alvarez, A., *The School of Donne*, 1961, London : Chatto and Windus.

Andreason, N.J., *John Donne : Conservative Revolutionary*, 1967, Princeton University Press.

Bald, R.C., *John Donne ; A Life*, ed. Wesley Milgate, 1970, Oxford University Press.

Bethell, S.L., *Shakespeare and the Popular Dramatic Tradition*, 1944, Westminster : P.S. King and Staples Ltd.

Bush, Douglas, *English Literature in the Earlier Seventeenth Century*, 1945, Oxford University Press.

Coffin, C.M., *John Donne and the New Philosophy*, 1937, London : Routledge and Kegan Paul Ltd.

Cruttwell. Patrick, *The Shakespearean Moment*, 1954, London : Chatto and Windus.

Chambers, E.K., ed., *Poems of John Donne*, vols. i and ii, 1896, London : George Routledge and Sons Ltd.

Duncan, J.E., *The Revival of Metaphysical Poetry : The History of Style—1800 to the Present*, 1959, Minneapolis.

Ford, Boris, ed., *From Donne to Marvell*, 1960, Penguin Books.

Fausset, H.I., *John Donne : A Study in Discord*, 1924, London.

Gardner, Helen, ed., *John Donne : A Collection of Critical Essays*, 1962, Prentice Hall.

———, *John Donne : The Divine Poems*, 1952, Oxford.

Garrod, H.W., ed., *John Donne : Poetry and Prose, with Izaac Walton's Life*, 1946, Oxford.

Gosse, Edmund. *Life and Letters of John Donne*, vols. i and ii, 1899, London.

Gransden, K.W., *John Donne*, 1954, London : Longmans, Green and Company.

Grierson, H.J.C., ed., *The Poems of John Donne*, (indicated in the foot-notes as *Donne's Poetical Works*), vols. i and ii, 1912, Oxford University Press.

Guss, D.L., *John Donne, Petrarchist : Italianate Conceits and Love Theory in the Songs and Sonnets*, 1966, Wayne State University Press.

Hamilton, K.G., *The Two Harmonies : Poetry and Prose in the Seventeenth Century*, 1962, Oxford.

Hayward, J., ed., *John Donne : Complete Poetry and Selected Prose*, 1930, London.

Hillyer, R.S., *The Complete Poetry and Selected Prose of John Donne and the Complete Poetry of William Blake*, 1941, New York : The Modern Library.

Hughes, R.E., *Progress of the Soul: The Interior Career of John Donne*, 1968, New York.

Hunt, Clay, *Donne's Poetry : Essays in Literary Analysis*, 1954, Yale University Press.

Jessop, A., *John Donne*, 1905, London : Methuen and Company.

John Donne : Concordance to the Poems, eds., Combs, C. Homer, and Z.R. Sullins, 1972, Hendricks House.

Leishman, J.B., *The Metaphysical Poets*, 1934, Oxford : Clarendon Press.

——,*The Monarch of Wit*, 1957, London : Hutchinson University Library.

Lewis, C.S., *English Literature in the Sixteenth Century*, 1954, Oxford : Clarendon Press.

Louthan, Doniphan, *The Poetry of John Donne : A Study in Explication*, 1951, New York : Bookman Associates.

Martz. L., ed., *Meditative Poem*, 1963, New York University Press.

Nelly, U., *Poet Donne—His Dialectic Method*, 1969, Connecticut.

Praz, Mario, *Studies in Seventeenth Century Imagery*, 1939, London : The Warburg Institute.

Redpath, Theodore, ed., *The Songs and Sonnets of John Donne*, 1959, London : Methuen and Company Ltd.

Sanders, W., *John Donne's Poetry*, 1971, Cambridge University Press.

Sharp, R.L., *From Donne to Dryden : The Revolt against Metaphysical Poetry*, 1940, Chapel Hill.

Simpson, Evelyn, *A Study of the Prose Works of John Donne*, 1924, Oxford, Clarendon Press.

Smith, A.J., *Songs and Sonnets by Donne : Critical Analysis*, ed., D. Daiches, 1965, New York.

Spenser, T., ed., *A Garland for John Donne*, 1931, Harvard University Press.

Stampfer, J., *John Donne and the Metaphysical Gesture*, 1971. New York.

Stein, Arnold, *John Donne's Lyrics : The Eloquence of Action*, 1962, London.

Tillyard, E.M.W., *The Metaphysicals and Milton*, 1960, London: Chatto and Windus.

Tuve,, Rosemond, *Elizabethan and Metaphysical Imagery*, 1961, Chicago : Phoenix Books.

Unger, L., *Donne's Poetry and Modern Criticism*, 1950, New York ; Russell and Russell.

Walton, I,, *The Life of Dr. Donne*, in *The Harvard Classics*, vol. xv.

Wells, H.W., *Poetic Imagery Illustrated from Elizabethan Literature*, 1924, Columbia University Press.

Willey, Basil, *The Seventeenth Century Background*, 1934, London : Chatto and Windus.

Williamson, G., *The Donne Tradition*, 1930, Harvard University Press.

————, *Seventeenth Century Contexts*, 1950, Faber and Faber.

————, *The Proper Wit of Poetry*, 1951, Faber and Faber.

Wilson, F.P., *Elizabethan and Jacobean*, 1946, Oxford : Clarendon Press.